NELSON

IN THE

CARIBBEAN

NELSON

IN THE

CARIBBEAN

The Hero Emerges, 1784–1787

Joseph F. Callo

Naval Institute Press
Annapolis, Maryland

Naval Institute Press
291 Wood Road
Annapolis, MD 21402

Library of Congress Cataloging-in-Publication Data
Callo, Joseph F., 1929–

   Nelson in the Caribbean : the hero emerges, 1784–1787 /
Joseph F. Callo.

        p.   cm.
   Includes bibliographical references and index.
   ISBN 1-55750-206-4

   1. Nelson, Horatio Nelson, Viscount, 1758–1805—Homes and
haunts—Caribbean Area. 2. British—Caribbean Area—History—
18th century. 3. Great Britain—History, Naval—18th century.
4. Great Britain. Royal Navy—Biography. 5. Admirals—Great
Britain—Biography .6. Caribbean Area—History, Naval. I. Title.
DA87.1.N4 C257 2002
359'.0092—dc21

                                        2002009788

Printed in the United States of America on acid-free paper ⊗
10 09 08 07 06 05 04 03   9 8 7 6 5 4 3 2
First printing

Frontispiece: Engraving of Vice Admiral Lord Nelson by R. Golding, from a portrait by
Lemuel Abbott. The painting was made after the Battle of the Nile when Nelson was
forty-three years old, and his career and fame were in full flood.

To my nephew, David Fontana, New York City firefighter,
who sacrificed his life on 11 September 2001

Greater love hath no man than this . . .

—JOHN 15:13

Contents

Foreword   ix

Acknowledgments   xv

PART ONE
THE PLACE

1   Pivot Point of a Career   3
2   World within a World   19
3   Sea of Contention   36
4   Local Perspective   48

PART TWO
THE TIME

5   Geopolitical Factors   63
6   Troubled Waters   76
7   Legal Morass   92

8	The Schomberg Affair	104
9	Fraud and Pardon	115

PART THREE
THE WOMAN

10	The Predecessors	127
11	A Young Widow	142
12	Courtship	153
13	Marriage	163
14	Aftermath	176
	Conclusion	189
	Chronology	197
	Notes	209
	Bibliography	217
	Index	223

Foreword

Which are the most formative years of a person's life? St. Ignatius Loyola is reputed to have said, "Give me a child until he is six and he is mine for life," and with my own sons I can see how their experiences in those first half-dozen years have contributed to shaping the fine young men they have become. Yet of course the first six years are by no means the only formative ones, and in their young manhood my sons, still changing and developing, know that their present experiences, choices, and decisions will continue to shape the rest of their lives.

In *Nelson in the Caribbean,* prize-winning author Joseph Callo focuses on the period which he persuasively argues was a much more important influence on Nelson's career than hitherto acknowledged, perhaps the most formative of Nelson's professional life. It was brief—just over three years, from March 1784 to July 1787—but packed with life-shaping experiences in which Nelson was obliged, often alone, to make choices and decisions that he knew would profoundly affect and possibly break his whole future career.

Perhaps the two most striking aspects of the period are Nelson's youthfulness and the huge weight of responsibility that was placed on his slight shoulders. He did not think himself too young, pointing out firmly to one of his much older critics that he was the same age as William Pitt, prime minister of Britain, "and think myself as capable of commanding one of His Majesty's ships as that Minister is of governing the State." He was indeed well experienced: By the time he sailed from England to his new command, he had been a full-fledged captain for nearly five years. Nevertheless he still seems astonishingly young for the tasks he had to face in the Caribbean. There, unless any more senior officer of the Royal Navy came on station, he was going to be responsible not only for a warship and her entire crew, but also for any and all naval matters and events that might affect British interests in every part of a six-hundred-mile crescent of islands, the Leewards and the Windwards—and he was still only twenty-five years old.

In analyzing how Nelson met the challenges and opportunities that came his way, Callo divides his text into three parts, "The Place," "The Time," and "The Woman," effectively presenting us with three extended, interrelated essays, each vital to the whole. Together they show the developing complexity of Nelson's character as he sowed the seeds of fame—and of notoriety, too.

Most days (perhaps every day) of his life in the Caribbean, the dominant thought in Nelson's mind was of choices and decisions: how should he act, and what would be the outcome? Throughout his period of command Great Britain was at peace, but the command was fraught with sensitive, difficult questions whose chosen answers could seriously affect a young man's career progress. While recognizing local needs, should he defy local wishes and uphold the Navigation Laws? Encountering infractions of discipline, whether from a seaman, a royal prince, or a retired commodore, should he be merciful, tactful, forceful? Armed only with inadequate orders from far away, should he seize the initiative, act now, and seek official approval later? Not least: should he marry?

If we apply imagination, placing ourselves in his often thankless situation and wondering what to do, it becomes terribly clear that sometimes these were genuine professional dilemmas, with no possibility of a good and safe outcome whatever we might decide. For Nelson those situations may have been the worst (damned if you do, damned if you don't), but at any rate he could follow his conscience. In all lesser situations there were at least two alternative courses of action; in every one, weighing the situation and being aware of the risks, he chose the more hazardous option. This was not because he liked risk for its own sake; rather it was because he was willing to accept risk, even very high risk, whenever he felt the safer alternative was unacceptable. In this regard, his Caribbean command showed him to be in some ways a most unusual (and in others a perfectly typical) young man of twenty-five, twenty-six, and twenty-seven years of age. If one had to choose a single word to summarize his developing character in 1784–87, it would probably be *resolute,* for he was remarkably resolute in all things, including courtship.

Had he been a little less resolute, what might have happened instead? Dividing these into certain, probable, and possible, the certain outcomes would have included the unnecessary death of at least one seaman, the continuation of a corrupt system of naval supply, and the progressive orientation of the Leeward and Windward islanders away from Great Britain and toward the United States. The probable outcomes would have included a much easier life for him during his command, much less reactive irritation within the British Admiralty, and consequently a far better chance of a new command after his return from the Caribbean, instead of five years' unemployment on half-pay.

By extension of that, had he been a little less professionally resolute in the Caribbean, the possible outcomes could have included the saving of his marriage; for if a tragedy emerged from his development in 1784–87, it was the failure of his marriage. His terse autobiographical comment on his wife Fanny, "by whom I have no children," may hint that her failure to conceive by him was the key, and it is true that he had a very strong fatherly streak. But that was written in October 1799, when—following his head-wound at his first sensational victory, the Battle of the Nile (1–2 August 1798), and his subsequent adulation in Naples—he was passionately in love with, and loved by, Emma Hamilton, wife of Sir William Hamilton, Britain's ambassador to Naples. Before then he had loved Fanny's son Josiah as his own, a factor that certainly influenced Fanny in their courtship, and although some of Nelson's language of courtship sounds stilted and formal today, there is no reason to doubt that at the time of his wedding, he was truly in love. Nor is there much reason to doubt that by the time he was allowed to return to sea, the bonds between him and his wife had already been fatally worn away, eroded by the effects on each of them of his exclusion from active duty.

So much for most of the outcomes, certain, probable, and possible, had he been a little less resolute in his time as the

Royal Navy's senior commander in the western Caribbean. But the fact is that he *was* resolute. People make mistakes of judgment, and in the course of his life Nelson made plenty, not least in the effects of his professional actions in the Caribbean upon one of his big dreams, that of a happy, stable marriage. Yet, as Callo makes clear, although Nelson engaged in no warlike combat during his Caribbean command, and although he generally hated being there, the experience was his proving-ground as a naval officer. Had he not been resolute then, there is one other certain outcome: he would not have become the brilliant combat commander of later years, seizing the initiative from opponents, daring to trust his own judgment, audaciously ignoring orders, and— by no means least—instilling in his officers and men an unbounded confidence in his personal care and leadership.

Thus it was that in the Caribbean, Nelson sowed the seeds of both fame and notoriety, accepting the risks of what he might reap. For us today, the scales of danger and the stages on which we play may be different, but the principle remains the same.

STEPHEN HOWARTH

Acknowledgments

I am indebted to Colin White for providing excellent input on this project, to Stephen Howarth for writing the foreword, and to Michael Nash for giving knowledgeable advice on the subject of Nelson. Ira Dye and Randy Mafit provided sound advice and welcome encouragement for my efforts, for which I thank them.

The Golden Cockerel Press graciously granted permission for me to use some of the wonderful artwork that appeared in its book *Nelson's Letters from the Leeward Island.* The staffs of the British Library, the National Maritime Museum of Greenwich, the Royal Naval Museum in Portsmouth, the New York Public Library, and the New York University Bobst Library were patient and responsive during my research. Lys Ann Shore brought exceptional professionalism to the book's editing. Image Quest Photographic Studio of Kansas City brought its creative talent to preparation of certain of the book's illustrations. Desmond Nicholson and the Antigua Museum provided information about Antigua, and the Nevis Historical and Conservation Society provided information about Nevis.

Finally and above all, I thank Sally, my wife, for her patience and encouragement.

PART ONE

The Place

The woodcut illustrations in this book are from *Nelson's Letters from the Leeward Islands and Other Original Documents in the Public Record Office and the British Museum,* an extremely limited edition published approximately fifty years ago by the Golden Cockerel Press, London. The illustrations help re-create both the physical and cultural environment in which the young captain of HMS *Boreas* operated between 1784 and 1787. The West Indies environment was a palpable—and unique— influence in the events of this pivotal period of Nelson's career.

One

Pivot Point OF A *Career*

He will one day astonish the world.

—SIR WILLIAM HAMILTON

"On last Friday I was commissioned for the *Boreas*, in Long Reach . . . and I am also sorry to say that the same day gave me an ague and fever, which has returned every other day since, and pulled me down most astonishingly."[1]

That matter-of-fact statement about his new command, with its quick and negative association with an ague and fever, was written from London on 23 March 1784 by then-captain Horatio Nelson. The letter was addressed to his former commanding officer and mentor, Captain William Locker. After the decidedly pessimistic beginning of his letter Nelson went on to say that he was going to be assigned to the West Indies; this definitely was not his first choice for his next tour of duty, and the letter lacked any of the enthusiasm that might be expected as a young captain anticipated a new command at sea.

RUN-UP TO THE WEST INDIES

Before his assignment to HMS *Boreas,* a 28-gun frigate, and the West Indies Station, Nelson had served an active tour as captain of HMS *Albemarle.* He began that assignment in 1782 with a trans-Atlantic convoy to Quebec, and following the delivery of the convoy he captured several prizes in the waters off the Canadian coast. Unfortunately—and for reasons never clearly established—the captured ships and their prize crews never reached port, denying Nelson the prize money the captures would have yielded. That financial loss would have an indirect bearing on his marriage a few years later on the Caribbean island of Nevis.

Also during Nelson's command of *Albemarle* he met and fell in love with a young woman in Quebec; the brief romance nearly had a disastrous impact on his naval career. Later in the course of his assignment in *Albemarle* he had occasion to meet Admiral Lord Hood and Prince William Henry; and each would be a factor in Nelson's West Indies tour of duty, in one case during the tour and in the other case in its immediate aftermath.

HIDDEN SIGNIFICANCE

When his orders to *Boreas* and the West Indies materialized, Nelson had been hoping for an assignment to the Jamaica Station, where he believed there was an opportunity for career-enhancing action. And if Jamaica was not to be his next duty assignment, then he hoped it would be the East

Indies, where he could serve under his friend, Commodore William Cornwallis.

But Nelson's initial lack of eagerness for the Caribbean assignment belied the importance of events to come in the West Indies. As it turned out, the assignment to *Boreas* marked the beginning of a unique three-year period in his career, a period far more important than it would appear from the limited attention it generally receives in accounts of his life. A more careful examination of that three-year span in Nelson's career leads to a new and expanded understanding of the naval officer who shaped the course of history from the decks of his ships.

Interestingly Nelson himself underplayed the significance of the period in his autobiographical "Sketch of My Life."[2] That brief account, written in 1799 for the *Naval Chronicle,* and then revised by the early Nelson biographers, James Stanier Clarke and John M'Arthur, in their 1809 biography, contained only two meager paragraphs about his West Indies assignment of 1784–87. And those two paragraphs touched on only one subject, his controversial enforcement of a series of maritime laws designed to protect British trade.

Omitted were a number of other noteworthy events, including a career-threatening controversy over his authority as second in naval command on the station; the courting of his future wife, Frances Nisbet; their marriage; his activities while Prince William Henry was serving as a captain under his command; and a troublesome pardon for a seaman sentenced to hang by a court-martial convened and headed by Nelson himself. Each of those events, and others that occurred during the same three years, was much more than a simple milestone along a career path. Each experience left an imprint on Nelson's character, and his reactions to the various circumstances provide clues to how he would behave as his career developed through more attention-getting phases in the future.

Tom Pocock, respected Nelson biographer, neatly captured how Nelson's tour in the West Indies both shaped and predicted his history-making life: "American waters made Horatio Nelson the man he became."[3] The Americas, according to Pocock, were the place where Nelson learned "to lead men and love women; to gamble for the highest prizes of fame and fortune with his own future as the stake." And although Pocock was referring in that discerning statement to an entire series of Nelson's early assignments in all of the Americas from Canada to the Equator, his observation has particular validity when applied to Nelson's assignment in the West Indies.[4]

BAD OMENS

The debilitating combination of ague and fever Nelson described to his friend, Captain Locker, was only the first of a series of disquieting events, incidents that set the tone for difficult situations in his approaching assignment. The second of those disagreeable events was, by any naval officer's view, one of a captain's worst nightmares. The ship's log indicates that the date was 11 April—with Nelson just recently aboard his new command, and shortly after they left Woolwich Dockyard in London—when a pilot ran *Boreas* aground. The embarrassment of the captain and his crew was compounded by the fact that at low tide it was possible for onlookers to actually walk around the stranded ship. A frustrated and angry Nelson referred to the agent of his anguish as "the damned pilot." But of greater importance than the palpable embarrassment of Nelson and his crew, sailors of the Age of Sail were notoriously superstitious, and the grounding surely would have been considered a bad omen by those preparing *Boreas* for her coming deployment.

Several weeks after that piloting misadventure Nelson wrote to the Admiralty from the Downs about a very different problem, one that occurred when he reached that anchorage on his way to Portsmouth from the Nore anchorage in the Thames estuary. He reported: "[S]ixteen of His Majesty's Subjects were detained by force, on board of a Dutch Indiaman, upon which I demanded and received them on board. The master of the Ship has refused, notwithstanding all arguments that I could make use of . . . to give up their chests, upon pretence they are in debt to the Ship."[5]

The situation Nelson described was politically sticky, the kind of unanticipated distraction a youthful and ambitious commanding officer definitely did not need as he readied his ship and crew for a transatlantic voyage to an important operational theater. As evidence of his own awareness of the potential for trouble in the diplomatically sensitive situation, Nelson hastened to add in his report to his seniors at the Admiralty that he was showing "every politeness and attention" to the Dutch captain.

Undeterred by the political sensitivity of the situation, Nelson immediately took firm action by cutting off all entrance to and egress from the Dutch ship. Then, after the fact, he sought official approval with a letter to the Admiralty. His reaction to the problem with the Dutch captain presaged his aggressive approach to immensely more serious political situations to come in the Caribbean, when again he would act first and seek approval afterward. This was a quickly passing but important example of a developing characteristic, one that involved immediately seizing the initiative in a situation, rather than waiting for official direction or further events to determine the course to be taken.

This inclination to snatch the initiative in circumstances ranging from legal matters to issues involving naval precedence was to be tested and then reinforced during the next few years in the Caribbean. And during those years that inclination would harden into an important element of Nelson's personality. Eventually, as Nelson's career developed, that element, combined with other developing traits, emerged as part of a winning battle doctrine. It was his combat doctrine, even more than Nelson's tactics, that carried him through the momentous victories he achieved during the historic final years of his career at the Battles of the Nile, Copenhagen, and Trafalgar.

On the same day that Nelson wrote to the Admiralty, the Dutch captain relented, and the chests were surrendered to their British owners. Nelson's quick and firm action achieved the desired results: The British seamen had their freedom and their belongings, and the Admiralty was spared a potentially awkward situation with a nation with which it had delicate relations.

Nelson's comment on the confrontation, in another letter to Captain Locker, anticipated some of the difficulties to come in his new assignment, and even of events to follow his command of *Boreas*. He wrote: "[T]he admiralty fortunately have approved my conduct ... a thing they are not very guilty of where there is a likelihood of a scrape."[6] This critical view of the Admiralty's frequent lack of support for captains willing to make difficult decisions on distant stations was penetratingly accurate. Over the course of Nelson's often-controversial career he found himself in a variety of career-threatening "scrapes." One such difficult situation was only a matter of months away, when he would set himself in rancorous opposition to the civilian officials, plantation owners, merchants, customs agents, and even his own naval commander in the West Indies.

STILL MORE BAD SIGNS

After reaching Portsmouth, there were more irritations. One was Nelson's own brother, Reverend William Nelson, who was convinced that he wanted to be a Navy chaplain and that Nelson should accept him in that billet in *Boreas.* Nelson had diplomatically but unsuccessfully tried to convince his brother that he was not cut out for life at sea, but he finally relented and signed him on as his ship's chaplain. As it turned out, the realities of a transatlantic voyage did what Nelson had failed to do: they convinced Reverend Nelson that his future lay ashore. As a result, William returned to England shortly after his arrival in the Caribbean, but for the short term, he was yet another nagging distraction for *Boreas*'s commander.

In addition—something else that Nelson had mentioned in his March letter to Locker—the wife of Admiral Sir Richard Hughes, Nelson's new commander-in-chief in the West Indies, along with their daughter and thirty supernumerary midshipmen, were among *Boreas*'s passengers for the month-long transit. On the one hand, Nelson, who always was attentive toward and protective of the midshipmen aboard his ships, probably did not mind having the additional young men underfoot. In fact, later in his letter of 23 March, he asked Locker, "[I]s there any young gentlemen you wish me to take?" On the other hand, he made it clear that he was not looking forward to weeks at sea with what he later referred to as the "eternal clack" of his admiral's wife.

To make matters worse, Lady Hughes was in a search mode to find a suitable husband for her less-than-beautiful daughter.

And that latter circumstance was a potentially career-bending situation for Nelson, who perhaps was the most attractive target of opportunity for the solicitous mother during the many weeks of their voyage. Adding to Nelson's irritation at having to carry Lady Hughes and her daughter to the West Indies was the considerable expense that he, as captain, had to bear to transport them to their destination. That it was common practice for a captain to bear such an expense was little consolation to one who lived on his modest Navy pay. As it turned out, however, Nelson's initial contact with the admiral's wife later paid important dividends.

Finally, as Nelson prepared for deployment, there was a somewhat bizarre event in Portsmouth that had nothing to do with seagoing matters. A horse Nelson was riding bolted, and after an uncontrolled gallop through the town and environs, Nelson was forced to leap from the saddle to prevent serious injury to himself or possibly even death. Perhaps the worst aspect of the situation was that he had been riding with a young woman whose horse also bolted and whom another young man rescued. Although visualizing the scene of Nelson aboard his uncontrollable mount has its humorous aspects, no doubt the damage to Nelson's ego was as real as the bruises to his back and leg resulting from his desperate leap to safety from the back of the frenzied horse.

After the foregoing series of events, all of which added up to an inauspicious beginning for Nelson's third frigate assignment, *Boreas* departed for the West Indies on 17 May 1784. And it is not difficult to imagine how those irksome weeks leading up to his departure for the West Indies could be unsettling to the ambitious young officer with a burgeoning professional reputation.

A CAREER ON THE RISE

Without a doubt Nelson was a rising star in his profession; he already had commanded three ships in His Majesty's Navy by the time he was appointed at age twenty-five to the command of *Boreas.* The previous commands included the brig, HMS *Badger;* the 28-gun frigate, HMS *Hinchinbrooke;* and the 28-gun frigate, HMS *Albemarle. Hinchinbrooke* was his first command as a post captain, a rank that he reached at the age of twenty.[7] Nelson's achievement of post-captain rank at that age was noteworthy for several reasons. First, he was somewhat young for promotion to that rank; second, he had as yet no significant seagoing combat experience, which was usually a prerequisite for promotion to post captain. That Nelson had reached that rank under those circumstances was an indication of his growing reputation for leadership and his high standing at the Admiralty.

The *Hinchinbrooke* and *Albemarle* assignments, plus his newly assigned duty in *Boreas,* gained membership for Nelson in the informal but highly regarded fraternity of eighteenth- and nineteenth-century British frigate captains, a special group of daring and particularly resourceful naval officers. Among those exceptional captains were such well-known naval heroes as Pellew of HMS *Nymphe,* Courtenay of HMS *Boston,* and Cochrane of HMS *Speedy.* Although he had not yet commanded a ship in combat, Nelson had earned noteworthy combat distinction during a previous Caribbean assignment, when he led the naval portion of an arduous, combined Army-Navy assault against the Spanish at Fort San Juan in Nicaragua in 1780.[8] The cooperation between Nelson and his Army counterpart during the attack on Fort San Juan was to represent the kind of interservice relationship he would seek, but not always find, in future combined Army-Navy operations.

Nelson's appointment to command of *Boreas* during peacetime, when so many of his brother captains were on inactive duty with half-pay, was yet another indication that his professional reputation was on the rise at the Admiralty. His brother William actually questioned how he had managed to secure such a command in a time of peace. Somewhat defensively Nelson replied that his assignment was based purely on his ability and reputation. His letter responding to William's question approached brotherly posturing: "[H]aving served with credit was my recommendation to Lord Howe, First Lord of the Admiralty. Anything in reason that I can ask, I am sure of obtaining from his justice."[9] Howe indeed was among the senior admirals of the British Navy who, throughout Nelson's career and despite his various detractors at the Admiralty, Whitehall, and the royal court, recognized that his unique qualities of leadership far outweighed the flaws in his personality.

AN ADDED POSITIVE FACTOR

Although there was some truth in Nelson's claim that his ability earned his appointment, almost surely there also was a degree of influence involved. For example, in addition to his official calls on Lord Howe at the Admiralty to appeal for command of a ship, he spent time socially with Admiral Lord Hood in London, and was even introduced at court by Hood. These social connections may have been even more important than his official appeals to the First Lord of the Admiralty.

Nelson had met and impressed Lord Hood when in command of *Albemarle* on the American Station. Hood, who recently had earned his title for his role in the British victory at the Battle of the Saintes, was impressed with Nelson's declared preference for a station where a captain could earn honor rather than prize money. After their meeting, according to Nelson, Hood had written to him "and promised me his friendship." That friendship of a senior officer in favor with both the Navy's and the nation's leadership could well have been the key to Nelson's command of *Boreas* and his assignment to the West Indies as second in naval command and senior officer afloat on that station.

The position of senior officer afloat, although an informal title, represented important recognition in its own right. In that capacity Nelson often was in operational command of the British ships on the station and was in a position to exercise considerable operational initiative. It was the kind of circumstance a young frigate captain would have relished. That assignment and the professional independence attached to it, as much as the command of a ship, provide evidence that Nelson was in favor where it counted at the Admiralty. He was marked as an officer with the potential to command more than a single ship—a critical distinction in a naval career. On a grander scale it was the kind of opportunity for independent responsibility that Nelson would later seek and receive from his future commanders-in-chief, particularly in the Mediterranean.

Nelson's assignment to the West Indies came in an era when influence (known as "interest") was an important factor in the career of every British naval officer. Many good officers failed to obtain promotion to post captain, or failed to secure career-enhancing seagoing commands after promotion to post captain, because of lack of interest at the Admiralty, Whitehall, or the royal court. Influence, or interest, counted in an officer's career right from the start. For example, it was a close family contact with his uncle, then-captain Maurice Suckling, that had earned Nelson, at age twelve, his initial berth as a midshipman aboard a ship of the line, HMS *Raisonnable,* which was commanded at the time by his uncle.

As he began his assignment as commander of *Boreas,* Nelson was, despite his young age, a thoroughly seasoned naval officer. Having entered the British Navy as a midship-man at an early age, he had already sailed in the Atlantic and Indian Oceans, as well as in the Baltic and Caribbean Seas. He had experienced combat ashore, and like many of his Navy brothers, when there was no Navy ship available, he sailed in the merchant marine. Experience in the merchant service increased his understanding of and respect for the ordinary seaman. In later years that understanding and respect gen-erated an almost fanatical loyalty among the lower decks in the fleets he commanded in momentous battles, a "force mul-tiplier" that paid crucial combat dividends. That exceptional loyalty is particularly noteworthy, given that many men in the crews of his ships had been forced into naval service against their wills by the notorious naval press gangs of the time.

OTHER CAREER INFLUENCES

In contrast, and notwithstanding Nelson's well-developed professional naval capabilities when he arrived in the West Indies on 26 June 1784, subtler aspects of his character were still in formation, including elements of leadership that were to mark his unique naval career. This is an important reason why the events of his *Boreas* command are worthy of greater attention than they have generally received. Indeed, during those three years some of the most interesting and critical aspects of Nelson's character, qualities that were to carry him to his position as a shaper of history, came to the fore and were reinforced.

Another noteworthy aspect of Nelson's three years in *Boreas* was that he was not involved in combat during that period. Britain was not at war, so there were none of the opportunities for combat experience that he had during other stages of his career. In Nelson's case, the opportunities for distinction in combat yet to come included hand-to-hand actions, single-ship actions, amphibious assaults, cutting-out actions, and major fleet battles. But in 1784 those dramatic battles in which he would gain crucial victories for his country were still over the horizon.

In one way Nelson at this time was representative of thousands of British naval officers during the Age of Sail: those who pursued successful careers in less than dramatic circumstances and without personal glory. Historian Richard Woodman described Britain's peacetime Navy as it existed immediately before and during Nelson's West Indies assignment, characterizing it as an institution that bore little resemblance to the history-shaping force it soon would become. "The Royal Navy of the day was not the instrument it was to become in the greater war now looming. It was riddled with corruption and jobbery, slack in its pursuance of its objectives, and rarely had sufficient ships in commission to accomplish its objectives."[10] Perhaps that detour on the British Navy's rise to preeminence as the naval force that dominated the sea in the nineteenth and early twentieth centuries is the reason why so many of Nelson's biographers have failed to focus on those three formative years in his career. In any event all three of the circumstances mentioned by Woodman—corruption, lack of clear mission objectives, and a shortage of ships—were experienced by Nelson during his tour in *Boreas.* The challenges and personal stresses that all three of those negatives precipitated were part of the tempering of his leadership qualities.

Despite the lack of opportunities to earn distinction in combat, Nelson's tour as commanding officer of *Boreas* was defining in other ways. Observing Nelson at this particular juncture in his career offers a unique window on his persona. It is a special opportunity to observe the early development of a leader who was not just a brilliant combat commander, but also one who learned to make a full range of command decisions. It is an opportunity to study the maturing of a leader as he learns to motivate those around him during the daily nitty-gritty of naval operations. We see him as a commander carrying out his ship's routine and his country's controversial and less than dramatic maritime laws. Perhaps most important, it is an opportunity to begin to know Nelson as a man, rather than a legendary hero of epic battles. Nelson's tour in *Boreas* allows us to see him for what he was as a person rather than for the events of his career, as dramatic as those events undoubtedly were.

THE SPECIAL QUESTION OF DUTY

As Nelson went about his assignments in *Boreas,* the question of defining one's duty was very much a part of his ongoing professional progress, particularly in terms of developing the full range of military leadership. For many, that definition is limited to the letter of one's orders. For Nelson, however, it was a more far-reaching issue; as we observe him in *Boreas,* we are able to see him unequivocally come to terms with the question and establish a clear, and at times controversial, pattern for the future.

The preeminent American sea-power prophet, Admiral A. T. Mahan, summed up the profound dilemma involved in the challenge to Nelson of defining his duty. In his biography of Nelson, he wrote: "It is difficult for the non-military mind to realize how great is the moral effort of disobeying a superior, whose order on the one hand covers all responsibility, and on the other entails the most serious personal and professional injury, if violated without due cause; the burden of proving which rests upon the junior."[11] Mahan's point is precisely relevant to what Nelson went through in *Boreas*. As he doggedly pursued the enforcement of the Navigation Acts, while simultaneously challenging his naval commander, civilian officials, and the local populace, Nelson addressed and settled this profoundly important issue. It is important to note that it was not his ego or a thirst for glory, or for that matter a blind drive to enforce a law for the sake of enforcement, that drove Nelson at this and later stages of his career. It was a reasoned and firmly anchored conviction that he was doing his duty to king and country.

FIRSTHAND EVIDENCE

Another noteworthy aspect of Nelson's three years in the West Indies as captain of *Boreas* is that much of what took place was recorded in his own writings. As a result, his firsthand views of the events of that time probably provide the best perspective on that period of his career. Certainly those accounts provide essential factual information, but more important, Nelson's own words provide insights that take us beyond what he did to what and who he was. In their biography of Nelson, Stephen and David Howarth point out this special dimension of his writings: "(H)is voice comes through clearly—chatty, warm-hearted and considerate, with an elegance of style derived from his own wide reading, and the rhythms of the King James Bible."[12] Those qualities still come through his words today, despite what might seem to be awkward syntax by today's standards. Nelson himself alerted us to the importance of his letters and dispatches when he referred to his words in a letter to a friend as "the inward monitor of my heart upon every difficult occasion."[13]

The three years that Nelson spent in the West Indies as commanding officer of HMS *Boreas* were intense. There was great stress as he aggressively pursued his duty in a way that made him a hated man among the islands' plantation owners and merchants. There also was great joy as he met, courted, and married an attractive and intelligent woman. In significant ways those events, plus others during the three years, set Horatio Nelson on the course that separated him from the many other outstanding officers in the British Navy of the time. As he strode the quarterdeck of *Boreas,* Nelson was doing more than pursuing his career; he was preparing to shape history.

What then were the events of his character-shaping tour in *Boreas*—a ship that triggers no images of glory, such as those associated with his historic battles fought in *Captain, Vanguard, Elephant,* and *Victory*—that had such profound impact on Nelson's life and career? The answers lie in three areas: the place, the time—and a woman.

Two

World WITHIN A World

Our ships were British oak. And hearts of oak our men.
—SAMUEL JAMES ARNOLD

HMS *Boreas,* Nelson's ship in the West Indies from 1784 to 1787, was truly a world in itself; it was the compressed core of the unique universe in which he would operate as the senior officer afloat on the station and develop as a naval leader destined for immortality. In the tight physical confines of the ship and its even more restrictive organizational limits, Nelson, his officers, and his crew lived out three years of their careers—and their lives. The ship, a Mermaid-class frigate built in Hull on England's Humber River, was one of the ubiquitous British Navy frigates that sailed the world's oceans during the eighteenth and early nineteenth centuries.

These multipurpose ships played an essential day-in-day-out role in applying Britain's naval power and making that power a determining geopolitical force during Britain's wars with revolutionary and Napoleonic France. By the end of Nelson's career Britain had more than two hundred of these naval workhorses in commission. In the latter stages of his career Nelson, as a fleet commander, would write on numerous occasions and with considerable emotion about the importance of the British Navy's frigates in his own operations. Perhaps the most memorable example followed his search for the French fleet bearing Napoleon to Egypt during June and July 1798.

During his frustrating hunt for that huge fleet, the warships of which he eventually tracked down on 1 August, Nelson was seriously hampered by his lack of frigates, and he wrote emotionally about the seriousness of the problem caused by that lack in his force. In a long letter to Earl St. Vincent in June 1798 he wrote about his search for Napoleon's fleet before the Battle of the Nile: "It then became the serious question, where are they gone? (Here I had deeply to regret my want of Frigates, and I desire it may be understood, that if one-half the Frigates your Lordship had ordered under my command had been with me, that I could not have wanted information of the French Fleet.)"[1] In another instance, as part of his follow-up reporting after he eventually destroyed the French battle fleet at Abukir Bay, he wrote to the Admiralty expressing his feelings in words that went well beyond normal official language (and that demonstrated his ability to write with impact): "Was I to die this moment, 'Want of Frigates' would be found stamped on my heart."[2]

THE FRIGATES OF NELSON'S ERA

Noted British author, and expert on the subject of frigates in the Age of Sail, Robert Gardiner summed up the performance requirements of these legendary ships: "Frigates . . . needed speed, seakeeping, manoeuvrability, strength, fire-power and capacity (for range), and all this had to be achieved within modest dimensions."[3] These multipurpose ships were used for handling convoy duty; gathering intelligence; scouting for major fleets; carrying out commando attacks and commerce raiding; serving on blockade; suppressing enemy privateers and pirates; carrying important dispatches; helping to salvage damaged ships-of-the-line after battle; conducting hydrographic surveys; showing the flag; suppressing what Britain considered to be illegal trade, and more. Nelson, during his tour as captain of *Boreas,* employed his ship for several of those functions, with particular emphasis on the suppression of trade between the British colonies in the West Indies and the former colonies to the north.

The frigates were not as heavily gunned as the ships-of-the-line that carried 50–100 or more cannons, but their 20–40 or more guns made them weapons platforms to be taken seriously by any potential enemy. Much of their duty involved independent operations, which generally suited ambitious and aggressive captains like Nelson, and command of one of these flexible and hard-working ships was both a challenge and a source of professional satisfaction. In many instances such commands were stepping-stones along a path to command of the more powerfully gunned ships-of-the-line, and ultimately, major naval squadrons and fleets; this was to be the pattern for Nelson's career. However, many of the best captains of the British Navy of Nelson's time continued to serve in frigates throughout most of their very successful careers.

A frigate on the West Indies Station was a severely compressed physical and psychological environment. Time ashore for the officers and crew was limited, and the ship was more than an important part of one's life—it *was* one's life. The routine was inexorable and based on one imperative, the needs of the ship. Rough weather and disease were constant threats, which took more lives during the Nelson era than combat did. Against all these lethal threats competence, exhaustingly hard work, and luck were the barriers. Despite those challenging, even threatening, aspects of life aboard a frigate in the West Indies, boredom and loneliness could corrode men's spirits. The tropical heat and humidity, especially the hammering sun, were debilitating, particularly for someone like Nelson who had grown up in England's much cooler Norfolk region. Extended periods of beckoning shorelines viewed only from the ship's rail were common, and at times the highly unpredictable mail was the only real link to the world outside the ship.

HMS BOREAS

Boreas, named after the Greek god personifying the north wind, was one of a group of frigates sometimes referred to as "The Early Frigates" or "The Small Frigates." Her length was a mere 125 feet and her beam was 34 feet. The Small Frigates were rigged with main-, fore-, and mizzenmasts, like the larger and more powerful frigates that came later in the Napoleonic Wars and the War of 1812. However, they lacked the heavier armament, as well as the design and construction refinements, such as iron fittings and water tanks, of the later, larger frigates. The Small Frigates of Nelson's day, with batteries of 20–28 guns, were labeled sixth-rate ships, and they were the smallest command for a post captain.

The Admiralty's labels for ship sizes at the time began with the sixth-rates and then moved up to fifth-rates with 32–44 guns, fourth-rates with 50–60 guns, third-rates with 64–80 guns, second-rates with 90–98 guns, and finally, first-rate ships with 100-plus guns. The first-rates were the massive, triple-gun-decked vessels, such as Britain's famous HMS *Victory,* the French *L'Orient,* and the Spanish *Santissima Trinidad,* which dealt out massive doses of death and destruction in the great fleet battles of the time.

Life definitely was not physically comfortable aboard *Boreas* during her three years in the Caribbean under Nelson's command. The heat and humidity were often worse than unpleasant; heatstroke and sunstroke were common. Below-deck spaces were extremely cramped, and there was little ventilation. The food generally was monotonous, and after extended periods without resupply, the fare could be barely edible. In the late summer and fall, hurricanes were a constant threat to both ship and crew. Spending the hurricane months in port, as was the common practice, was no guarantee of safety, as ships at anchor could be driven ashore by the ferocious winds of even low-level hurricanes.

Rats, cockroaches, and mosquitoes came in waves in the tropical environment. Space was at a premium; stores, at times for up to six months, had to be accommodated; guns and ammunition also consumed a lot of space, as did the spare sails, cordage, anchoring tackle, and boats. Frequently livestock for food was carried aboard. What space was left was for "living."

As captain, Nelson had his own quarters, which meant that he lived in relative comfort. Also as captain, he had a modicum of privacy. At the same time he was psychologically more isolated, by far, than anyone else in his ship, and his correspondence to his future wife and others shows that he frequently suffered from that isolation. On a day-to-day basis, his detachment from those around him in *Boreas* meant that he lacked the routine interpersonal contacts that somewhat mitigated the stress of life for others aboard a ship of the British Navy. And because of his power—at times up to and including the power of life and death—he was feared. When he was on his ship's quarterdeck at sea, he had his own space, the entire windward half of that area. It was a space with invisible but palpable barriers. The entire ship's crew, even the officers on watch, penetrated those barriers only at the captain's invitation or for official purposes.

Nelson's responsibilities as captain were as awesome as his power; they included the lives of the approximately two hundred crew members, the safety and material condition of the ship, and—most important of all in the eyes of his seniors at the Admiralty—the success of his missions. Because his assignment in the West Indies placed him thousands of miles from the Admiralty, he often had to make important and potentially controversial decisions without specific orders covering the situation at hand. Making those decisions involved considerable risk to his career.

Yet another complication caused by the tyranny of distance under which Nelson operated was that his intelligence was often late and inaccurate. Frequently, because of the uneven quality of his intelligence, he was forced to act upon little more than guesswork. This added stress to an already challenging assignment.

Notwithstanding all the circumstances that rendered decision-making difficult, Nelson could be admonished by the Admiralty or even court-martialed for what was deemed to be an error of omission just as quickly as for a perceived error of commission. For example, in one instance toward the end of his West Indies tour, when he failed to secure particular authorization from his seniors before diverting HMS *Pegasus* to Jamaica on her way back to Britain, the Admiralty reprimanded him for both transgressions simultaneously.

In light of his willingness to depart from orders during his later career, noteworthy examples of which are embedded in the Nelson legend, Nelson's response to that particular letter of admonition from the Admiralty has to trigger a smile: "I beg you will inform their Lordships that I duly observe the contents of it; and they may be assured that in future no consideration shall ever induce me to deviate in the smallest degree from my orders." Nelson himself probably looked up and smiled at some point as he penned those words and then sent them on their way to his land-bound leaders living and working in relative comfort in London.

On the positive side, it appears that *Boreas* performed well for Nelson, at least up the end of his tour, when wear and tear inevitably took a heavy toll on the ship's physical condition. The Admiralty records for her class of frigates suggest that she was probably a better than average performer when sailing to windward, but not particularly fast when before the wind. Her maneuverability was probably good but not exceptional. Nelson and his senior officers would have thoroughly understood all these nuances of *Boreas*'s performance characteristics.

Nelson's dispatches and letters contain few, if any, complaints about her seaworthiness, and there are several references to the ship being well-found, as well as being manned with good officers and men. For example, in a letter from London to his brother William in March 1784, he wrote: "I am told she is a very fine ship." Later, upon his arrival at Madeira on 7 June 1784, en route to the West Indies, he described the initial phase of his transit as a "pleasant passage," despite his collection of burdensome passengers. Then in September of the same year, he wrote to Captain Locker from Antigua referring to *Boreas* as "well Officered and manned." An orderly, well-found, well-sailed ship provided a special satisfaction for those whose livelihoods—and lives—depended on her capabilities on a day-to-day basis. It should also be noted, however, that toward the end of his West Indies tour Nelson sensed disaffection among the crew.

In contrast to exaggerated modern depictions of life in Nelson's Navy in print and film, life aboard ship was less brutal than often portrayed. There were harsh aspects to the discipline and living conditions, to be sure, and it was in general a physically and mentally hard existence. But the same was true for life on land, and aboard *Boreas* there was a counterbalancing factor. Unlike some of his brother officers, Nelson saw discipline as a means to an end, not an end in itself. Another positive aspect of Nelson's leadership was his recognition of the direct correlation between a busy operating tempo, continuous activity for his crew, and good morale. When the ship was under way, there were constant training exercises; when in port, in addition to the endless maintenance work, amateur dramatic performances and other activities were regular events. Nelson also understood and acted upon the growing realization in the British Navy that there was a strong connection between the quality of the diet and the general health of the crew; generally his crews were healthier than average for the time, and he took great pride in that accomplishment.

As a result of his focus on the well-being of his crew, one of the constants of Nelson's career was the exceptional loyalty, even affection, felt for him by the most hard-bitten of those men. When, for example, Nelson's previous command, HMS *Albemarle,* was paid off, virtually the entire crew volunteered to serve in his next command. This evenhanded leadership and genuine concern for his crews were qualities that would have made the negative aspects of *Boreas*'s duty in the Caribbean significantly less onerous.

THE SHIP'S ACTIVITIES

Like all of the British Navy's ships during the period of the wars with revolutionary and Napoleonic France, including the brief interludes of peace, *Boreas* was worked hard during her West Indies deployment. After her arrival at Barbados on 26 June 1784, it would have been rare, except for unusual circumstances and the hurricane season, for the ship to be at any one island for an extended period of time. There was a considerable amount of territory to be covered on an ongoing basis: The chain of islands in the general area encompassed by Nelson's activities covered a distance approaching a thousand nautical miles. The island chain included the Virgin Islands (what today are both the U.S. and British Virgin Islands), St. Maarten/St. Martin, St. Barthélemy, Barbuda, St. Kitts (also called St. Christopher), Nevis, Antigua, Montserrat, Guadeloupe, Dominica, Martinique, St. Lucia, St. Vincent, Barbados, Grenada, and others. Although many of the islands looked similar from the sea, each had a personality of its own.

Within the islands in Nelson's operational area, Britain, France, Spain, Holland, Denmark, and other nations vied for control, or else, lacking control, sought significant leverage that might lead to control. Yet getting from point to point in a square-rigged ship on that demanding station could be frustratingly slow. In some wind and weather circumstances it was downright impossible, and the only recourse was simply to wait for a change in the weather conditions.

Some of the ship's activities were quite predictable, others less so. Among the predictable were such necessary activities as securing food and water; training in combat evolutions, such as gunnery; seeing to the routine maintenance of the ship; and carrying out basic hydrographic investigations. In November 1784, for example, Nelson wrote to Captain Locker that he was on his way "to examine a Harbour said to be situated in the Island of St. John's, capable, it is supposed, to contain a Fleet of Men of War during the hurricane seasons. . . . it is said here to belong to the Danes."[4] Those who sail the waters of the U.S. Virgin Islands today will find an anchorage at the eastern end of St. John called Hurricane Hole that is still used as a protected anchorage during hurricanes. Its depth and size would indeed have accommodated a significant number of men-of-war in the eighteenth century, and it was probably the anchorage referred to by Nelson in his letter to Captain Locker.

Emergency ship repairs for problems ranging from a blown-out sail to a sprung mainmast to hull damage caused by striking reefs or rocks were dealt with as they occurred, and they happened frequently. Although the shipyards of the West Indies were not comparable to those of the British Islands, several could accomplish significant maintenance and repairs to square-rigged ships. Antigua, Nevis, and Barbados were among the islands visited for repairs and routine maintenance. In September 1785, for example, Nelson wrote that his ship was being "hove down" in English Harbour, Antigua.[5]

As captain of a British ship on a station where he was second in command, Nelson also recognized an official social side to his duties. Much of his correspondence of the time describes both the events and his feelings about this aspect of his West Indies assignment. For example, in a letter in January 1787 from Antigua to his wife-to-be in Nevis, Nelson describes a breathtaking social schedule: "Today we dined with Sir Thomas, tomorrow the Prince [Prince William Henry, the future King William IV] has a party, on Wednesday he gives a dinner in St. John's, tomorrow the regiment, in the evening is a mulatto ball, on Thursday a cock fight [and] dine at Col. Crosbie's brother's and a ball, on Friday somewhere but I forget, on Saturday at Mr. Byam's the President [of the Council at Antigua]. If we get well through all this I shall be fit for anything."[6] Nelson, like most professional naval officers, would have viewed such an intense social schedule as an annoying distraction from his professional assignments.

BUILDING AN INFLUENTIAL FRIENDSHIP

A special feature of Nelson's social activities involved his two-sided relationship with Prince William Henry. The prince was captain of HMS *Pegasus,* which was assigned to the West Indies during the end of Nelson's tour there. He had advanced at a rapid pace from the rank of midshipman to post captain, unquestionably on the basis of his royal status. The prince came under Nelson's command as the senior officer afloat on the station. Yet at the same time Nelson acted as an aide to the prince because of his position as a member of British royalty. Prince William was a direct military subordinate of Nelson in the West Indies, and it stands to the credit of both men that their friendship continued, with varying degrees of intensity, throughout Nelson's career. The situation required a deft balancing act on Nelson's part, which his correspondence indicates he managed to maintain, perhaps with some compromises on the military chain-of-command side of the equation. In any event, William's royal status complicated Nelson's position of command authority among the ships with which he operated in the West Indies.

One of the most important factors working in Nelson's favor in regard to Prince William was that the Prince had met Nelson shortly before his assignment to the West Indies, and had formed a positive opinion of him. The occasion of that meeting was a visit by Nelson, then captain of HMS *Albemarle,* to HMS *Barfleur,* when that ship was anchored off Staten Island in New York harbor in 1782. Prince William himself described that initial meeting: "There was something irre-sistibly pleasing in his address and conversation; and an enthu-siasm, when speaking on professional subjects, that showed he was no common being. . . . as for prize money, it never entered his thoughts. . . . I found him warmly attached to my Father, and singularly humane: he had the honour of the King's ser-vice, and the independence of the British Navy, particularly at heart."[7] Prince William's characterization of Nelson as he was perceived just before his tour in *Boreas* touched on many of the personality factors that drove Nelson's actions in the West Indies between 1784 and 1787. One carryover of the prince's positive initial impression of Nelson was his later insistence that he be the one to give the bride away when Nelson and Frances Nisbet were married on the island of Nevis in 1787.

BEYOND THE ROUTINE

Any presence of a possible future enemy provided a distinct change of tempo for *Boreas*, and one such occurred when a French frigate, with an unusual number of senior military offi-cers aboard, appeared in March 1786 while *Boreas* was anchored at Nevis.[8] Nelson had been alerted to the presence of the French ship in the area, presumed to be surveying the local islands' coastal waters and fortifications. The day after their initial appearance Nelson found the French anchored off St. Eustatius, then in Dutch control, and he proceeded to anchor his own ship about four hundred yards off their quarter.

After reciprocal salutes Nelson and his officers were invited ashore by the Dutch governor for a dinner with their opposite numbers from the French ship. During dinner, Nelson politely offered to escort the French during what they were attempting transparently to characterize as merely a cruise among the British islands; his offer was declined emphatically. Nelson was undeterred by the French rejection of his suggestion, however, and proceeded to accompany the French frigate as she began to move among the islands. The French abandoned their activities after a few days of such close surveillance by *Boreas,* and returned to Martinique, whence they had come.

Two aspects of the encounter with the French frigate are noteworthy. The first is that Nelson acted aggressively without seeking orders from his commander, Admiral Hughes. He assessed the situation and immediately took the action that served his overall mission. Second, the incident carried a personal price for Nelson. After the event he suffered from serious headaches, which he attributed to having been in the sun for long periods during the several days of shadowing the unwelcome French frigate. The aftereffects of such overexposure to the sun, although they would not have been precisely diagnosed in Nelson's time, would have had a long-term effect on his health.

A terse entry in *Boreas*'s log for 13 November 1784 revealed a very different kind of unscheduled event, something that occurred among those whom he often referred to as "my children." The entry read: "Four of the Midshipmen went on shore and fought a duel, when Mr. Stansbury wounded Mr. Andrews mortally." In his nonofficial description of the event, Nelson commented that, if Andrews had died, the survivors of the duel would have been subject to court-martial and possibly hanging. It was clear that Nelson strongly disapproved of such means of settling personal disputes, and there would have been no allowances for the young age of the participants in the duel. Fortunately for all parties, Andrews, who actually was the brother of a young woman whom Nelson had courted before his departure from Britain in *Boreas,* survived his wound and went on to become a post captain.

Overall, Nelson's vigorous enforcement of Britain's Navigation Acts undoubtedly was the most significant of his nonroutine activities, and this aspect of his tour was to become one of the most revealing and strongly formative features of his three years in the West Indies. In January 1785 he wrote from Guadeloupe that "[t]he longer I am upon this Station the worse I like it. Our Commander has not that opinion of his own sense that he ought to have. He is led by the advice of the Islanders to admit the Yankees to a Trade; at least to wink at it."[9] Those few lines foreshadowed dangerously stormy political weather to come for Nelson in the Caribbean. His actions during those circumstances were to illuminate, and to reinforce, important facets of his character.

THE MATURING OF A PROFESSIONAL FRIENDSHIP

Not the least among the events of Nelson's tour in *Boreas* were the various activities he shared with his friend and professional colleague, Cuthbert Collingwood. The two had met as midshipmen and then served as lieutenants in the same ship early in their careers, when Collingwood replaced Nelson in HMS *Lowestoffe.* On other occasions during their lives, Collingwood continued to follow Nelson. And in the end it was Vice Admiral Collingwood who led the British lee column alongside Nelson's line into battle against the French-Spanish Combined Fleet at Trafalgar. The pattern continued after Nelson's death, when Collingwood assumed command of Britain's Mediterranean Fleet after Nelson was killed at Trafalgar.

When Nelson arrived in the West Indies in *Boreas,* Collingwood was already there as captain of the frigate HMS *Mediator.* In a letter to Captain Locker of September 1784, Nelson referred to his reliance on his friend's abilities: "Collingwood is at Granada, which is a great loss to me."[10]

Later, in March 1786, Nelson reflected the warmth of his friendship with Collingwood by describing him as "an amiable good man" and "a valuable member of society."[11] The maturing relationship between the two captains included the social side of their assignment in the West Indies as well as the professional naval side. That extra dimension featured an interesting mutual friendship with Mary Moutray, the wife of the commissioner of the naval dockyard on Antigua.

However, it was in the professional naval aspects of their assignment, and particularly those associated with the contentious enforcement of the Navigation Acts, that the bond between the two was most strengthened. Those enforcement efforts were extremely unpopular among the British administrators, merchants, and plantation owners of the islands. Collingwood, together with his younger brother Wilfred (who died while the three were together in the Caribbean), stood virtually alone alongside Nelson to stop the trade between the newly independent America and the British colonies of the West Indies. Although Nelson seemed to bear the brunt of the local reaction and lawsuits, it was Collingwood who first took action to stop the trade that was in violation of the Navigation Acts.

In January 1785 the governor of the Leeward Islands wrote to the British secretary of state: "As Captain Collingwood had not communicated to me the receipt of any order for what he had done, I was rather at a loss to account for the motives of his conduct."[12] Virtually at the same time Nelson was hastening to join his friend in the conflict. He wrote to his commander, Admiral Hughes: "[A]t a time when Great Britain is using every endeavour to suppress illicit Trade at Home, it is not wished that the ships upon this Station should be singular, by being the only spectators of the illegal Trade which I know is carried on at these Islands."[13] It was a matter of the two young captains standing against powerful civilian opposition, and the indecisiveness of their own military commander, to do what they perceived as their duty. The sense of frustration and isolation during those events surely drew the two men closer in friendship and professional respect.

The strength of this relationship grew as their respective careers developed. Ten years after their tours of duty in the West Indies, Nelson and Collingwood fought side by side again, this time in combat, in the Battle of Cape St. Vincent in February 1797. That victory marked the start of Nelson's national fame as a combat leader. After Nelson had covered himself with glory at that event, he wrote to Prince William Henry, by then the duke of Clarence, of his close friend, who had supported him at a crucial point in the conflict: "Captain Collingwood disdaining the parade of taking possession of beaten enemies, most gallantly pushed up, with every sail set, to save his old friend and messsmate, who was to all appearances in a critical situation."[14] Even in the final chapter of his career at Trafalgar, Nelson was praising his friend "Col" as he took his column into action alongside his own.

Nearly another decade later, in 1805, Collingwood, in a turnabout of sorts, wrote to the duke of Clarence in praise of his friend Nelson, who had been killed during the British victory at the Battle of Trafalgar: "The loss which your Royal Highness and myself have sustained in the death of Lord Nelson, can only be estimated by those who had the happiness of sharing his friendship. He had all the qualities that adorn the human heart, and a head which, by its quickness of perception and depth of penetration, qualified him for the highest offices of his profession."[15] As in Prince William's earlier assessment of Nelson, Collingwood had fixed on some of the truly exceptional qualities of his friend and professional colleague, qualities that had been factors as they worked together in the face of significant difficulties to carry out their duties in the West Indies.

Appropriately, in a final career parallel, both Nelson and his friend Collingwood were laid to rest in the crypt of St. Paul's Cathedral, London, Nelson in 1806 and Collingwood in 1810. It was during the politically stressful events of their simultaneous tours on the West Indies Station that their exceptional friendship came to maturity. Although it was a relatively subtle influence on Nelson's career, his strong friendship with Collingwood became a significant element in Nelson's development as Britain's most celebrated naval hero.

Three

Sea OF Contention

The English planters were encouraged to settle there
to maintain the islands for Imperial purposes.

—JAMES ANTHONY FROUDE

When Nelson dropped anchor in Carlisle Bay, Barbados, at the end of June 1784, he had arrived in a theater of operations of considerable strategic importance. For years political control in the West Indies had ebbed and flowed among the world's colonial powers, and the eastern rim of the Caribbean, where Nelson operated between 1784 and 1787, was a challenging environment for a British frigate captain of the time. There were opportunities for personal growth and career advancement, and there were risks with career-ending implications. The events that would determine whether it would be growth and advancement or devastating errors for Nelson were played out against an extremely complex Caribbean background.

EARLY INFLUENCES

In Columbus's report of his first voyage of discovery he wrote: "I have taken possession for their Highnesses by proclamation and display of the Royal Standard without opposition." From that report in 1493 of the establishment by Columbus of the first European settlement on Hispaniola, the Caribbean was a compact maritime arena for fierce colonial struggles. Today almost all the islands, most of which now have benign, tourism-based economies, have their reminders of the military component of those struggles over the course of the sixteenth, seventeenth, and eighteenth centuries. In some cases centuries-old, stone plantation work buildings have been converted into "charming" architectural accents in chic resorts. In other instances ruined fortresses or rusting cannons still point seaward, toward old enemies that have long since disappeared over the horizon. The contestants in the formerly lethal competition for imperial power included the British, Danish, Dutch, French, Portuguese, Spanish, and other European nations.

Three very different motivations drove the earliest colonizers: accumulation of gold and silver for both national and personal wealth, religious conversions, and raw adventure—usually in that order. In Columbus's report to King Ferdinand and Queen Isabella about his first voyage to America, for example, there are several references to gold and precious metals, including one about "numerous mines of metals" and another, much more appealing, about "magnificent rivers, most of which bear gold."[1] One of the results of this initial emphasis on the extracting of gold and silver was an early failure by Columbus and others among the first European explorers to found permanent colonies. They extracted mineral wealth, rather than establishing enduring economic viability in permanent communities.

Following Columbus's initial discoveries, it was audacious British sea captains such as Sir John Hawkins, Sir Francis Drake, and Sir Henry Morgan who initiated an English presence among the lush islands of the Caribbean. Although at times it was difficult to distinguish these captains from the pirates who infested the region, they were the critical players in wresting the early imperial domination of the West Indies from Spain. They did so despite the political inconsistencies of the British government in London. The name of the tiny corner of the Caribbean surrounded by today's British Virgin Islands, known as the Sir Francis Drake Channel, provides contemporary evidence of that successful early British presence, and some of the modern nautical charts of the area are based on centuries-old hydrographic surveys conducted by those early British navigators.

MATURING CONCEPTS OF POWER

By Nelson's time the emphasis in the Caribbean was following the pattern developing in other regions of the world. During the three hundred years between Columbus's initial discovery and the late eighteenth century, maturing concepts of maritime power based on trade had come to equal and then surpass the desire for plunder, missionary conversions, and the excitement of exploration by sea. More powerful and more complex commercial forces inexorably overshadowed cruder colonial motives throughout the lands discovered by European explorers; the Caribbean was typical in this regard.

Embedded in that change was a growing understanding that permanent, economically strong colonies, plus strategically located naval bases and dockyards, were vital elements of national economic and military power. This was particularly true for Britain, as an island nation with a rapidly developing merchant class, a mercantilist foreign policy, and an affinity for the sea. During this phase of Caribbean history many people in Britain considered the West Indies to be the most precious possessions of the empire. At the end of the nineteenth century and the beginning of the twentieth that growing understanding of maritime power would be articulated by sea-power visionaries Admiral A. T. Mahan in America and Sir Julian Corbett in Great Britain.

As economic influences became more important in the contest for colonies, there was a continuing change of control of the islands that rimmed the eastern Caribbean, including the West Indies. Britain, France, the Netherlands, and Spain played leading roles in the cycles of conquest, loss, and reconquest. St. Kitts, Nevis, and Montserrat, for example, were taken by the French and then subsequently returned to British control shortly before Nelson arrived in the West Indies. A little-discussed by-product of those constant changes of national control among the islands was the influence of such instability on the local economies of the colonists, which already were subject to the vagaries of the tropical weather and often marginal soil conditions.

Many of the cycles of military conquest were marked by naval actions, but in general, none of those naval actions was conclusive enough for one nation or another to establish enduring political and military control of the region. The action off Grenada in July 1778, between the French fleet of Admiral d'Estaing and the British force of Admiral Byron that had pursued the French fleet across the Atlantic, as well as the action between Admirals Guichen and Rodney near St. Lucia and Guadeloupe in 1780, offer examples of such strategically indecisive battles. These naval actions are of interest to students of naval tactics in the Age of Sail, but they did little to radically change the larger strategic relationships in the Caribbean. Up to the point of Nelson's arrival in the West Indies in the summer of 1784, however, Britain and France, although certainly not the only players, had gradually emerged as the principal opponents in the ebb-and-flow struggles for Caribbean conquests.

THE BATTLE OF THE SAINTES

The Battle of the Saintes in April 1782, shortly before Nelson reached his West Indies assignment, rose above the others in strategic importance. That naval action did tip the balance in the region, and thus significantly shaped the political and military scene that Nelson would encounter on his arrival. The battle, between a British fleet led by Admiral Sir George Rodney and a French force led by Rear Admiral Count François de Grasse, was fought off a group of small islands between Guadeloupe and Dominica, called the Îles des Saintes, at various times referred to as "The Saintes" or "The Saints." The engagement, which was the first major sea battle of William Pitt the Younger's eighteen-year term as Britain's prime minister, has not received attention by naval historians comparable to that devoted to those actions fought at the same general period in the Atlantic and Mediterranean. The Battle of the Saintes did, however, create a pivotal shift in the West Indies in favor of Great Britain.

De Grasse was covering a large convoy, including troop ships. His fleet was heading to join up with a Spanish force committed to a combined French-Spanish attack on Britain's

Jamaica colony, which appeared to the French to be ready for the taking. When Rodney caught up with De Grasse, the British had a 36-to-30 advantage in numbers of ships of the line. That numerical advantage was the result of a British strategy of maintaining a marginally adequate "fleet in being" in home waters to forestall an invasion by France, as well as a reduced naval presence in other theaters. With those minimal forces elsewhere, Britain concentrated on strengthening its naval presence in the West Indies in order to force the military issue there with France. In addition, the French fleet had lost several ships of the line in collisions before the battle.

As a result of the fortuitous combination of Rodney's numerical advantage, a shift in the wind, the British tactical cohesiveness and superior gunnery, the effective use of the smashing effect of the newly introduced carronades, and questionable tactical maneuvers by the French, the British achieved a significant victory. The French loss of only five of their thirty ships of the line did not reflect the full impact of the event.

Noted naval and military historian Peter Padfield recognized the importance of this little-discussed victory: "The Battle of Chesapeake Bay, or Virginia Capes, had been the turning point of the American war; the Saints marked the turning point in the world war: it re-established the perception of British naval ascendancy lost since the Seven Years War, saved Jamaica . . . [and] threw the French service into an orgy of recrimination and self-doubt."[2]

Significantly, the crucial British victory at the Battle of the Saintes coincided with the financial fatigue experienced by both the British and French governments during their ongoing conflicts. By this time the financial stresses on the governments of the two nations were becoming intolerable. By 1789, for example, the French were spending nearly half of their national revenue on interest on their government's debt. In Britain's case, interest on the debt was consuming approximately two-thirds of the country's tax revenue. Although Britain's financial system was to prove considerably more resilient than that of France, dealing with a national debt growing from the nearly continuous struggle between the two countries was still an important issue in London. Against that background of debt, productive colonies—which were significantly more secure as a result of the Battle of the Saintes—became increasingly important in contributing to Britain's economic base.

PEACE AMONG BRITAIN, FRANCE, AND SPAIN

Britain, France, and Spain signed a peace treaty at Versailles on 3 September 1783, largely as a result of those financial stresses; it was the same day that Britain signed the Treaty of Paris ending the American Revolution. The Versailles treaty, and the Battle of the Saintes that influenced the shape of that agreement, left Britain as arguably the strongest force in the West Indies, notwithstanding the grip of other nations on individual islands in the area, such as the French on Martinique and the Dutch on St. Eustatius.

Based on his correspondence at the time, it appears that Nelson had few militarily threatening contacts with any of Britain's past and future enemies on his station. His actions toward those non-British enclaves mostly appear to have fallen into the "diplomatically correct" category. However, the British ascendancy and French self-doubt that the Battle of the Saintes and the treaty of 1783 precipitated had to be significant factors in Nelson's general state of mind as he began his duties in the Caribbean, only a year after the treaty was signed. He could feel confidence in his own professional abilities, which had steadily been reinforced during the events of his early career, and in the ascending naval power of his nation.

From another perspective, however, those same circumstances contained some potential career negatives for Nelson. For example, he would find few, if any, opportunities for combat glory or prize money in the West Indies. Several years before his arrival there, he had referred to the West Indies as "the station for honor," rather than for prize money. Times and circumstances had not changed, at least in terms of the lack of opportunities for prize money, by the time he arrived there in *Boreas*. Those conditions required Nelson to push his active mind, confident nature, and generally combative approach in directions other than actual battle.

COMBAT BY OTHER MEANS

If the actual combat between the French and British was suspended during the period immediately following the treaty signed at Versailles in 1783, there was no lack of other types of contention between the two governments. For example, although the difficulties associated with the respective national debts were different—France was still an absolute monarchy, while Britain was governed by a more open parliamentary system that limited the role of its monarchy—both nations heavily relied on foreign trade and economically productive colonies to regain fiscal equilibrium. That reliance forced Britain to place continued and heavy emphasis on ocean commerce; anything or anyone threatening that commerce was a target of the British Navy.

Further, the emergence of America as a new commercial competitor, particularly in ocean-borne trade, immensely complicated matters in the West Indies for Britain. After achieving independence from British rule, American merchants aggressively began to reestablish trade with the nearby markets of the West Indies; lumber, whale oil, tobacco, tar, and foodstuffs all were shipped south from the new United States. Immediately following the American Revolution, the foodstuffs were particularly important to Britain's West Indies colonies. Coffee, sugar, molasses, and rum were carried north on the return voyages, with sugar being particularly important. According to British law, however, this trade was illegal under the Navigation Acts.

The series of laws called the Navigation Acts, initially enacted under the rule of Oliver Cromwell, was designed to ensure the commercial stability of British merchants and shipbuilders, while also creating a reliable pool of skilled seamen and a viable British merchant marine. In addition, the acts were intended to assure a favorable balance of trade for Britain, and eighteenth-century British colonies were expected to play a positive role in maintaining that favorable balance. For many, particularly those in the power centers of London who did not have to directly face the economic vagaries of the region, it was expected that patriotism and strong social and cultural ties would motivate compliance with the Navigation Acts among the West Indies colonists. As it turned out, however, economic factors were paramount for the local plantation owners, many of whom were absentee landowners, and the local West Indian merchants.

In specific terms the Navigation Acts forbade direct trade in the West Indies by any but British ships manned by British seamen. Clearly Nelson understood the importance of protecting Britain's trade, and he accepted that noncombat role as an important part of his assignment, perhaps the most important part, given the lack of armed conflict in the area. He went so far as to remind political leaders in London in no uncertain terms of that aspect of his assignment; in June 1785 he wrote a memorandum directly to the king pointing out that the Navigation Acts were "most shamefully evaded" in the West Indies. Nelson focused on stopping those evasions with a stubborn determination that would characterize much of his official behavior in the West Indies.

GATHERING CLOUDS

Nelson's stubborn determination was clearly apparent, for example, in a letter to his military superior in the West Indies, Rear Admiral Sir Richard Hughes. The letter, written in January 1785, only months after his arrival on the West Indies Station, described the Navigation Acts in blunt terms as instruments "upon which the wealth and safety of Great Britain so much depends."[3] Nelson further showed his understanding of the importance of Britain's trade in a letter to the British secretary of state, written in November 1785: "We know that commerce is the enricher of every Country; and where She flourishes most, that will be the greatest Country."[4] These statements and others like them indicate that Nelson's approach to enforcing the Navigation Acts went well beyond a blind drive to enforce the law. He understood the strategic and economic basis of the laws, and pursued his duty despite the local economic stresses that were caused among the islands by his actions. For him it was, as it would be later in his career, a matter of concentrating on the largest issue involved.

An additional aspect of the Navigation Acts issue for Nelson was his residue of animosity toward America, which raised the emotional content of the situation for him. To Nelson the Americans were rebels who had been unfaithful to their homeland; on that basis they deserved to be denied the benefits that would accrue from being part of the British Empire, benefits from which they had separated themselves by armed revolution against their king and homeland. In the "Sketch of My Life" written by Nelson in 1799, he summed up his basic assessment of the situation at the time: "The Americans, when colonists, possessed almost all of the trade from America, to our West Indies Islands: and on the return of Peace, they forgot, on this occasion, that they became Foreigners, and of course had no right to trade in the British Colonies."[5]

A likely element of Nelson's animosity was the paternalistic attitude in Britain toward the Americans—a fact of life that had been a significant factor in the American revolt against Britain. The harsh treatment in America of royalists who did not flee to Canada after the conclusion of the American Revolution further raised the level of British resentment toward the former colonists. On 24 October 1784, shortly after his arrival in the Caribbean, Nelson wrote to his brother William, touching on the royalist issue: "From Barbadoes I am to go to the Virgin Islands to examine them, by a particular order from the Admiralty. I suppose they wish to find some good lands for the poor American loyalists."[6]

Nelson further revealed his general attitude toward the former subjects of the king a year later, when he wrote to Lord Sydney, then–secretary of state: "To see American ships and Vessels, with their Colours flying, in defiance of the Laws . . . loading and unloading in our Ports, was too much for a British Officer to submit to. I could not even by a tacit acquiescence suffer a Commerce so prejudicial to Britain to be carried on, legal or illegal: I was fully determined to suppress it."[7]

Those and other similarly strong statements suggest that Nelson's enforcement of the Navigation Acts went beyond his understanding of the importance of protecting the maritime base of Britain's power. They reveal an emotional extension of the war with the American revolutionaries that had just recently been concluded by Britain, but definitely not forgotten by Nelson. It was an emotional ember that was an ongoing factor in his actions, a situation that would be repeated later, in a greatly magnified form, in Nelson's hatred of France, and particularly of Napoleon as the personification of the excesses of the revolutionary republican government in France.

Four

Local Perspective

*The sole end for which mankind are warranted, individually
or collectively, in interfering with the liberty of action
of any of their number, is self-protection.*

—JOHN STUART MILL

The plantation system was the economic foundation of Britain's West Indies colonies during Nelson's tour in *Boreas,* though it was a somewhat shaky foundation. In consequence, the colonists' view of the Navigation Acts was very different from Nelson's. They saw those laws as impediments to the two-way trade with North America on which the viability of their plantations depended. For them those laws were one more threat to their economic survival. Beyond the threat to their livelihood represented by any restriction of their trade with the new United States, the growing abolitionist movement in Britain provided yet another dimension to their difficulties. As a result, the West Indies gentry, notwithstanding their political loyalty to the British Crown, were motivated by powerful, short-term economic factors—immutable realities that were in sharp conflict with Nelson's aggressive commitment to enforcing the Navigation Acts.

TWO DIFFERENT PERSPECTIVES

The same trade that Nelson perceived as illegal and detrimental to the greater interests of Britain was a matter of economic survival for the British plantation owners and local merchants, who considered any law that threatened their well-being as onerous and unfair. The similarity of the West Indian colonists' attitudes to those that had pushed the colonists to the north over the brink of revolution was striking, and Nelson did not fail to make comparisons between the two groups. At one point shortly after his arrival, he noted: "The residents of these Islands are American by connexion. . . . They are as great rebels as ever were in America, had they the power to show it."[1]

A compelling argument can be made, however, that the West Indian colonists were not restrained from revolt only by their lack of means, as Nelson suggested. He had to deal with rage but not rebellion, and as he went about his duties he encountered none of the overt acts of political defiance that had characterized the run-up to the Declaration of Independence in America. Strong cultural and social ties, combined with a strong reliance on Britain for military protection from other nations and growing threats of slave rebellions, made the colonists Nelson was dealing with very different from their counterparts to the north. But that was a distinction Nelson apparently did not make.

Another aspect of Nelson's difficult relations with the West Indian colonists concerned the colonists' economic unity.

Despite the significant political differences among the individual islands that made up the West Indies Station—and there were many such differences—the common reliance of so many of the people on the survival of their plantation-based economies was a strong unifying factor. As a result, the local opposition to Nelson's enforcement of the Navigation Acts was widespread, which made him, at times, not only extremely unpopular among the islands but even for weeks a virtual prisoner aboard his own ship. At such times he literally could not step ashore without the probability of being arrested and jailed. At one point, he wrote to his future wife about being "so much out of temper with this island [Barbados] that I would rather sacrifice anything than stay," a sentiment that was repeated on numerous occasions and about other islands as well as Barbados.

The effect of this social ostracism for doing what he perceived to be his duty surely was formative. It hardened Nelson for future personal difficulties with his military and political leaders over how he interpreted his duty, and coincidentally with British society over his later, flagrant love affair with Emma Hamilton.

CIVILIAN AND MILITARY LEADERSHIP

Although each of the islands in the West Indies maintained some de facto autonomy because of its geographic separation from the other islands, there was an overall colonial government in place to represent the Crown. The governor, sometimes referred to as the captain-general, usually resided on Antigua. The lieutenant governor was located on St. Kitts, and the president of the council lived on Nevis.

The commander-in-chief of the West Indies Station, Nelson's immediate military commander, was Rear Admiral

Sir Richard Hughes; it was Hughes's wife and daughter who had been transported from England to the West Indies by Nelson in *Boreas*. Hughes's command was located ashore at yet another island, Barbados, where he lived, to the consternation of many, in a boardinghouse. There his focus appeared to be as much social as military. And as events turned out, Admiral Hughes provided little support for Nelson when he needed it most on the West Indies Station. In the critical stages of what became a politically and legally dangerous confrontation for Nelson between himself and the local planters, merchants, and civilian administrators, Admiral Hughes wavered between siding with the local populace against Nelson and providing reluctant support to his second in command on the station.

This was not to be the only time Nelson had an uneasy relationship with an immediate military superior. For example, in 1799 Nelson refused the direct order of his immediate superior, Admiral Lord Keith, to detach certain ships from Naples to other locations in the Mediterranean. Nelson claimed that it was more important for him to protect the Kingdom of the Two Sicilies, one of Britain's most important allies in the Mediterranean, from Napoleon's armies. Others felt that it was the influence of Lady Hamilton in Naples that prompted Nelson's blunt refusal to detach the ships.

Yet another example of Nelson's departure from orders from his superior occurred when he was second in command to Admiral Sir Hyde Parker in the British fleet that defeated the Danes at the Battle of Copenhagen in April 1801. At the height of combat Nelson ignored Hyde Parker's order to break off the fighting between Nelson's squadron and the Danes. In this instance Nelson used his blind eye as an excuse for not obeying the signal from his commander-in-chief, claiming with grim humor that he could not see the signal, which was in clear view.

CONFLICTING AUTHORITY

Complicating the problem with Admiral Hughes was the blurring of the critical paths of authority on the West Indies Station through unclear lines of responsibility. Customs agents, who in some instances simply were corrupt, resented, and at times openly challenged, Nelson's authority to enforce the Navigation Acts. The Navy had no direct authority over those recalcitrant civilian officials. In yet another situation, the resident dockyard commissioner of Antigua, Captain John Moutray, who coincidentally was a naval officer on inactive duty, claimed military status that would have made him Nelson's military senior in the immediate area of Antigua. Nelson challenged the commissioner's claim, which had been precipitated by an order from Admiral Hughes actually establishing local military authority for Moutray. Eventually the Admiralty upheld Nelson's refusal to recognize Moutray's military authority, but in the short term the incident further strained his relations among the West Indies civilian leadership and with his naval commander.

Still another problem with the senior civilian leadership in the West Indies involved a confrontation between Nelson and the governor-general of the Leeward Islands, General Sir Thomas Shirley. Shirley and other officials in the West Indies began sending letters to the effect that the individual administrators in the islands were to make the decisions concerning which ships would be admitted to trade. Nelson at one point wrote to Captain Locker how he had "trimmed up and silenced" the general.[2]

In their 1809 biography of Nelson, authors Reverend James Clarke and John M'Arthur described an oft-repeated exchange between Nelson and General Shirley, who told Nelson during their confrontation that "old generals were not in the habit of taking advice from young gentlemen." Nelson's rejoinder was cutting: "I have the honour, Sir, of being as old as the Prime Minister of England, and think myself as capable of commanding one of His Majesty's Ships as that Minister is of governing the State."[3] Nelson's response was the kind that might have "trimmed up and silenced" the general, and coincidentally provided a memorable anecdote for his biographers, but it also was the sort of wounding remark that would have made permanent enemies, unobtrusive antagonists who would be in a position to damage his career at later stages.

A MATTER OF PERSONALITIES

In analyzing Nelson's difficulties with Admiral Hughes, Captain Moutray, and General Shirley, there is a temptation to dismiss his three antagonists as old, stupid, and possibly even corrupt. After all, they hindered Nelson in his attempts to carry out his duties as the senior officer afloat on the station, and they did so on what could be described as flimsy grounds, at best. Such a conclusion, however, would be, on the evidence, erroneous.

All three men had respectable, perhaps even distinguished, military careers. All were genial and were widely accepted by the local populace in their positions. Perhaps most telling, Nelson maintained a genuinely warm social relationship with all three, notwithstanding his official, and at times heated, differences of opinion with each of them. No evidence of corruption ever appeared. And even in his harshest criticism Nelson did not suggest that there was any deliberate dishonesty in the actions of Admiral Hughes, Captain Moutray, or General Shirley.

What can be concluded, when one gets beyond the temptation to demonize anyone who opposed arguably the most revered naval officer of modern history, is that the confrontations primarily were clashes of personalities. Nelson's antagonists were fairly easygoing administrators who were strong on getting along with those they had to deal with in local communities. Nelson, in contrast, was a rising star in the British Navy, one who was motivated by powerful principles, driving ambition, and an unshakable conviction of the correctness of his official positions.

In a penetrating analysis of the situation, Michael Lewis wrote that Nelson, in contrast to his three opponents, was "a furiously angry, highly patriotic young officer" at the time.[4] That volatile combination continued to ignite periodically after Nelson left the West Indies. The anger may have moderated somewhat with time, but the patriotism only accelerated as the threats to the British Navy and Britain by revolutionary France and its stunningly successful leader, Napoleon, steadily increased after Nelson's return to England in 1787.

THE GEOGRAPHICAL AREA AND ITS CONDITIONS

Nelson, his contemporaries, and his biographers refer to the general area in which he operated between 1784 and 1787 as the Leeward Islands or the West Indies—the terms were used interchangeably—most commonly the Leeward Islands. Based on Nelson's actual operations in *Boreas,* however, the more accurate term is the West Indies, the more inclusive of the two geographic areas and the one that includes both the Leeward and Windward Islands, extending from the Virgin Islands at the north to Grenada at the south. From his correspondence, we know that during his command of *Boreas* Nelson spent various amounts of time in Antigua, Barbados,

Deseada, Dominica, Guadeloupe, Montserrat, Nevis, St. Eustatius, St. John, St. Kitts, and Tortola. And without a doubt, in the course of his three years in the West Indies, he visited other islands as well. From the same correspondence we also know that other ships in his command operated as far south as Grenada.

Like other oceanic areas, the West Indies have a particular range of sailing conditions that would have influenced operations while Nelson was there. These conditions included the general weather patterns, navigation factors, and the wind. The overall weather patterns generally would have been benign for sailing ships; seasons are not as sharply distinguishable as in the temperate zones, and the temperature range generally is 70–85°F or 20-plus to 30°C. Nelson and most of his crew were acclimated to the northern temperate zone, and the semitropical climate of the West Indies, particularly the powerful sun, could make daily life uncomfortable and, at times, physically dangerous.

The winds generally come from a direction between northeast and southeast, being more northerly, and stronger, in the winter months, and more southerly, and less strong, in the summer months. Atlantic storms, particularly in the winter, would have created significant swells from the north. These swells would have made some otherwise good anchorages uncomfortable for days at a time, or for some periods even untenable. Periodically, even during generally good weather, line squalls would have moved through the islands where Nelson was operating. At times a succession of these brief but intense and drenching storms would have moved through the same area during a twenty-four-hour period. Those squalls would have generated wind gusts in excess of 30 knots, but in general, they would have posed no real threat to a well-found and well-manned ship. Particularly during December, fair-weather winds of more than 40 knots could have blown for several days without letup.

Most of the time, particularly in daylight, eyeball navigation was the rule for Nelson and the captains serving with him. Reefs and rocks could be dangerous, however, particularly at the entrances to anchorages, and in the eighteenth century charts could contain significant inaccuracies. Access to a local pilot was one of the best assets that a captain who did not have intimate knowledge of a specific area could have.

Undoubtedly the biggest single weather factor for Nelson while operating in the West Indies was the hurricanes. From July through October these tropical storms, with winds that could exceed 125 knots, were a potentially lethal danger; accordingly, operations for Nelson's small group of ships were restricted during those months. The danger from hurricanes was not eliminated in port, where many anchored ships were driven aground by these powerful cyclonic disturbances.

TWO SPECIAL ISLANDS

Antigua and Nevis, two of the Leeward Islands, played particular roles during Nelson's West Indies assignment. Antigua was the largest of Britain's possessions in the Leeward Islands at the time, and was considered to be the main base for the British Navy in the area. Many people saw it as the gateway to the Caribbean, since it was strategically located in relation to the major sailing routes in the region. The British were the first to colonize Antigua, and by the mid–eighteenth century it was the headquarters for the British governor of the Leeward Islands. It also was the site of English Harbour, a major dockyard for Nelson's ships and the other British ships in the area.

Nelson spent considerable time at Antigua, much of it at Windsor, the home of the dockyard commissioner, John Moutray. It was at Windsor that Nelson met the commissioner's wife, Mary Moutray, who became a close friend to both him and his colleague Captain Cuthbert Collingwood. Today elements of the dockyard remain at English Harbour, along with a Nelson museum, but nothing tangible remains of Windsor.

Nevis was another island that played an ongoing role in Nelson's West Indies assignment, particularly toward the end of his tour. There he spent time courting his wife-to-be at Montpelier, the plantation home of her uncle, who was president of the Nevis Council. The ruined foundation of this once-magnificent Caribbean home can still be seen, and one of the two stone gateposts that mark the overgrown location bears the inscription: "On this site stood Montpelier House, wherein on the 11th day of March 1787 Horatio Nelson, Then Captain of HMS *Boreas,* was married to Frances Herbert Nelson." The church where the marriage was recorded, St. John's Church, also known as the Fig Tree Church, still stands as an active center for religious worship and as an additional reminder of the important event in the lives of the young captain of HMS *Boreas* and the young widow of Montpelier that occurred there. Three miles to the north of Montpelier along Nevis's eastern shore was the town and harbor of Charlestown, where supplies for the plantations and merchants entered, and sugar, molasses, and rum from the plantations were shipped out. It was at Nevis that Nelson, early in his West Indies tour, impounded four American cargo vessels that were in violation of the Navigation Acts. The legal battle that ensued was one of the test cases for Nelson's policy of strict enforcement of the acts, as well as for his inclination to define his duty for himself.

THE PROBLEM OF INSUFFICIENT MEANS

There is little doubt that from the British point of view the Navigation Acts clearly proscribed direct trade between

America and the British colonies in the West Indies. It is just as clear that the American traders and their would-be partners in the British colonies of the West Indies felt differently. The American John Adams summed up the tightly linked interests of the United States and the British West Indies when he wrote that in the event of another war between the United States and Britain, "the West Indies would now declare for us if they dared."[5] For Nelson, however, there was a troublesome problem, well beyond the political, that affected his ability to fully carry out his duties in that respect: On a day-in-day-out basis he simply lacked the naval assets needed for full enforcement of the acts. As the captain of a frigate operating independently, or as the commodore of the tiny squadron he commanded at times, there was no way he could adequately cover his station so as to consistently prevent violations of the acts.

This was particularly true since the local populace participated in the violations. In terms of enforcing the Navigation Acts, and despite his own determination and Britain's status as the world's leading naval power, Nelson's mission exceeded his means. On occasion he wrote about the limits placed upon his naval means, surprisingly often, given the circumstances of his duties, in matter-of-fact terms.

Nelson's dilemma of having an assignment that exceeded his naval capabilities was not unique; it has been a problem for as long as naval forces have been used as instruments of governmental policies, while being built to meet budgets. He was in a position that many other naval officers had faced and would face, and he could have just gone along with the situation. Doubtless many of his fellow officers would have done just that and suffered little criticism. But Nelson's aggressive attempts to carry out his duty, notwithstanding the personal unfairness to him that was involved, were a product of both his stubbornness and his willingness to take political risks to pursue his duty as he defined it. One of the most astonishing aspects of his career, perhaps as amazing as his survival in scores of large and small combat situations, was his survival of the numerous political "scrapes" he precipitated by this stubborn pursuit of his duty as he saw it.

PART TWO

The Time

Geopolitical Factors

He who commands the sea has command of everything.

—THEMISTOCLES

*I*n his internationally influential book *The Influence of Sea Power upon History 1660–1783*, then-captain A. T. Mahan described Britain's geopolitical position in 1763, at the end of the Seven Years War: "The one nation that gained in this war was that which used the sea in peace to earn its wealth, and ruled it in war by the extent of its navy, by the number of its subjects who lived on the sea or by the sea, and by its numerous bases of operations scattered over the globe."[1]

The global circumstances of the Seven Years War described by Mahan led to Britain's development of the geopolitical strategy that carried it to ultimate victory over revolutionary and Napoleonic France. Some elements of that strategy were already firmly fixed when Nelson arrived on the West Indies Station. For example, the colonial plantation system was solidly established as the economic base in the area, and that system was closely linked to the politics and culture of the area. In addition several dockyards existed among the islands. Yet the full naval capabilities, in terms of the number of ships required for the overall strategy, were still in process of formation when Nelson arrived in 1784. All these circumstances surely influenced him as he began his tour.

It was a time of peace, at least superficially, between Britain and France. But also it was a time of intense struggle between the two nations—an epic economic, cultural, and philosophical competition, based largely on empire building, that would return the countries to armed conflict within a decade. But for the time being it was an eighteenth-century version of a "cold war." Professional naval officers who were able to see beyond their immediate duties—and Nelson certainly was one—knew it was only a matter of time before the contentious peace returned to lethal, global combat.

For Nelson, as the captain of a British warship and the senior officer afloat in the West Indies, there was no real peace interlude to be enjoyed. There was only the pursuit of the conflict by other means, and Nelson's actions and his correspondence bore out his awareness of the general environment in which he would be operating.

In May 1784, just before he departed for the West Indies, Nelson wrote to Captain Locker: "[H]ostilities must commence soon again with the French." And in January 1785 from Guadeloupe he complained to Locker about how serious a threat the American trade in the West Indies would represent, "are we ever again embroiled in a French war." Nelson's understanding that a return to war with France was imminent, and his conviction that American trade in the West

Indies would be a serious handicap in such a war, would have raised the stakes in his pursuit of his duty during his West Indies tour.

THE STRATEGIC PICTURE

By the late eighteenth century, when Nelson in *Boreas* was operating in the West Indies, it could justifiably be said that Britain's international influence reached to the 6-fathom curve off any landmass in the world. Reliance on that maritime reach repeatedly had proved to be a sound basis for Britain's steady rise in global influence over many years and many shifts in the global balance of power.

Where and when Britain's reliance on that maritime strength failed, it arguably was not because of any faults in the British inclination to leverage its maritime strength. Nor was it because of any lack of bold and capable naval leaders, like Nelson and his brother officers, who could carry out that strategy; there were many highly motivated and extremely professional officers in Britain's naval service. After the Battle of Trafalgar off Cadiz in 1805, the defeated French admiral, Pierre Villeneuve, commented on that human naval resource in a colorful observation: "To any other nation the loss of a Nelson would have been irreparable, but in the British fleet off Cadiz, every captain was a Nelson."[2] One might argue that as good as Nelson's naval colleagues were, they did not rise to the level of his genius as a leader. But there could be no argument that the overall quality of the British Navy officers of Nelson's time was exceptionally high, not just in professional skill but in fighting spirit as well. The latter characteristic was the critical enabling element in Britain's developing blue-water strategy.

In the instances where Britain's maritime power failed, it was because the naval means—a sufficient number of

deployed ships to implement a winning maritime strategy—
were not provided by the government in power. Arguably the
most striking, combat-related example of such a circumstance in the period following the Seven Years War was the
Battle of the Chesapeake, where the British, notwithstanding
the general power of the British Navy at the time, simply did
not have naval numbers adequate to the local situation. At
that dramatically decisive moment in history, Britain did
indeed have the "best" navy in the world. However, after the
entry into the war by France in 1778, the resources of that
powerful navy simply weren't equal to the immediate circumstances off the Virginia Capes in September 1781. The
general problem, in unvarnished terms, was that there were
too few ships to cover too many requirements.

That weakness could not be overcome by Britain's significant naval technological advances, such as the coppering of ship bottoms and the use of the carronade naval gun.
As a result, the hard-pressed army of the British at Yorktown
was not relieved, and General Cornwallis's surrender was
the result. A critical naval shortfall at a pivotal time and
place spelled defeat with far-reaching national implications
for Britain. The irony of the situation was that the fledgling
U.S. Navy was not even remotely comparable to the British
Navy at the time. It took a French fleet, imposed at a critical time and place in support of America's land forces, to
prevent the relief of Cornwallis and seal a geopolitical dis-
aster for the British.

Historian Paul Kennedy neatly summed up the British problem at the Battle of the Chesapeake: "The surrender of
Cornwallis at Yorktown was the direct result of that draining of
vessels from the American station, which permitted De Grasse's
superior squadron to block the Chesapeake. . . . Because she
[Britain] had insufficient strength to be superior everywhere

and because she dared not withdraw from any of the four main theatres—the Channel, Gibraltar, the West Indies, the American seaboard— then she ended up by being too weak in every one of them."[3] Historian David Syrett described British naval policy at the time as a "strategy of detachments," a series of ongoing, chess-like moves of fleet segments intended "to maintain naval superiority in distant regions, such as the West Indies and Western Atlantic, by sending detachments of ships overseas in pursuit of enemy naval forces."[4] Naval historian John B. Hattendorf brought the British problem into sharp focus with a single sentence about the British admiral at the battle, Sir Thomas Graves, whose "failure to defeat the French fleet and dislodge them from the Chesapeake to allow the British to bring reinforcements from New York was, in Washington's words, 'the pivot upon which everything turned.'"[5]

DIRECT IMPACT ON NELSON

On a smaller, local scale and in a noncombat context, this recurring problem for nations that try to do too much with too little in the way of naval resources was a factor in Nelson's West Indies assignment. Britain had dramatically reestablished its naval preeminence in that militarily strategic and economically vital arena at the Battle of the Saintes. And while Britain kept a major fleet in the theater, the British were able to exercise decisive naval control there. For example, in 1781 Admiral Rodney dispatched four frigates to Tortola to drive off a squadron of American privateers threatening that island. That was the kind of mission—short of a major battle but requiring a fleet large enough to spare four frigates for an independent mission—that was required for sea control in the immediate theater. Such an assignment realistically could not have been undertaken by Nelson in *Boreas* or, for that matter, by one of the tiny squadrons that he periodically commanded among the islands of the West Indies.

Unfortunately for Britain, after Rodney's fleet achieved its victory at the Saintes in 1782, his fleet could not be left for long in the West Indies; circumstances in other theaters were more pressing. The result was that on a day-to-day basis, only a few frigates, operating independently or in small squadrons with brigs and sloops, were left to maintain the sea control in the West Indies that had been achieved in combat by a major fleet.

As the senior officer afloat, Nelson occupied a strategically important position, but he did so with resources that certainly could not be expected to deal with a major unfriendly fleet or even a high tempo of multiship, noncombat missions. In the event, those resources were not even sufficient for a totally effective and ongoing enforcement of the controversial Navigation Acts—so closely related, in Nelson's conviction, to Britain's maritime and commercial power.

In a narrative of his difficulties in enforcing the acts, probably written at the end of June 1786 to Prince William Henry, Nelson described the problem: "As by Law, I could not lay by and see these Foreign Vessels trade, which they would most certainly have obtained leave to do, had they any communication with the Shore, I constantly turned them away without allowing them to land. But whenever the Ship was absent, the Ports were filled, and upon the Man-of-War's coming in sight, they cut or slipped and got away."[6] For Nelson, as a dedicated professional naval officer with a grasp of global strategic issues and a lingering distrust of the newly independent America, those circumstances would have been extremely frustrating.

SOME OF THE POLITICAL PLAYERS

The policies of the British governments of the period following the Seven Years War, including the years when Nelson was pursuing his duties in *Boreas,* involved the growing, if not always constant, recognition that Britain's main strength in the ongoing struggle with France would be its maritime power. Like any other aspect of history, the political dynamics were driven by an array of key players, people who shaped the policies that deployed naval leaders like Nelson were expected to carry out. Some of those political players earned brightly illuminated niches in history, others have receded into the shadows.

One of the principal architects of those policies was the Fourth Earl of Sandwich, who was First Lord of the Admiralty from 1771 to 1782, during the prime ministership of Lord North. Although his name doesn't exactly reverberate down the halls of history, Sandwich had much, both good and bad, to do with the policies that eventually evolved into Britain's blue-water strategy of the late eighteenth and early nineteenth centuries. He eventually lost his position as the civilian leader of Britain's Navy as the result of the British defeat in the American Revolution. But he was successful in guiding the Navy through that difficult period—a time when the Navy was being required to do too much with too little—and positioning it for the coming life-and-death struggle with revolutionary and Napoleonic France. If he presided over the loss of Britain's most potentially valuable colonial possession, he also positioned the British Navy for the bigger, more strategically crucial war to come.

Sandwich fought against the neglect of the British dockyards, which was just one of the British Navy's serious shortcomings during the American Revolution. As a result of his efforts, Britain was able to maintain a minimal shipbuilding and repair infrastructure that, although inadequate during the American Revolution, was at least capable of being expanded to support the country's sea-based strategy during the coming armed struggles with France.

In addition, Sandwich was instrumental in stretching Britain's naval resources to successfully use a small "fleet in

being" to hold off an invasion of the British Isles, while sending a major fleet to the West Indies to meet the French there.
That deployment to the West Indies indicates the very high
strategic value placed on that region by the British at that
time. Noted nineteenth-century British naval theorist Sir
Julian Corbett described Sandwich's strategy: "The West
Indian area, in which lay the enemy's principal object, was
treated as the offensive theatre and the home waters as the
defensive."[7] As a result, Admiral Rodney was able to fashion
his strategically important victory over the French at the
Battle of the Saintes. The strategy, however, fell short of permanently stalemating France's imperial impetus, which
would gain almost irresistible momentum under Napoleon.

But most important, by the time Sandwich left his position as First Lord of the Admiralty in 1782, the British Navy
had regained a small overall numerical advantage over the
combined naval strength of the French and Spanish. In a
practical context that quantitative superiority over the potential naval threat to Britain allowed the Navy to more significantly capitalize on its technological advances, such as the
coppering of ship bottoms and the widespread installation of
the highly effective carronades. In a more sweeping context,
the achievement of a numbers level that approached the
strategic requirements of the geopolitical realities established
the British naval momentum that ultimately ended the ex-
pansion of France in that era.

Peter Padfield characterized Sandwich as a "man of sound
sense and integrity."[8] It was that "sound sense" that prevented
the Navy's serious decline in numerical strength and naval
infrastructure from passing the point of no return. As a
result, his successor was able to begin rebuilding the more
powerful naval force Britain would require. In the meantime
the tiny force that Nelson had at his disposal may not have

been everything that he needed for his missions, as he perceived them, but at least the influence of the British Navy of the moment established a positive day-to-day naval environment in the West Indies. In that environment Nelson was able to think proactively, rather than reactively, notwithstanding the limited number and size of the British ships on the station.

William Pitt the Younger, who was appointed prime minister in 1784, at age twenty-four, was another of the leading architects of policies that affected events in the Caribbean during Nelson's tour there. In contrast to Sandwich, Pitt earned a prominent place in British history. Initially he focused on maintaining peace, achieving debt reduction, and fostering economic growth. But of immediate relevance to Nelson, Pitt, as a member of parliament before becoming prime minister, raised one of the issues—probably the most important issue—relevant to Nelson's West Indies command.

Pitt understood the economic dilemma of Britain's West Indies colonists and had proposed a bill "for the purpose of revising the beneficial intercourse that existed before the late American War, between the United States and the British Sugar Islands."[9] The bill would have facilitated the desperately needed trade between America and Britain's West Indies colonies. Unfortunately for the West Indian merchants and plantation owners, however, a government commission decided that there would be no exception to the Navigation Acts, notwithstanding the economic distress that set of laws was bringing to the British colonies in the wake of the American Revolution. Pitt's failure to secure relief for the British West Indian colonists from the economic strangulation of the Navigation Acts left Nelson in a politically dangerous position.

The commission's decision did not eliminate differences between advocates of strict application of the Navigation Acts for the sake of Britain's broad strategy and those, like Pitt, advocating a pragmatic accommodation of the economic realities of the merchants and plantation owners of the West Indies. Because it left unresolved the very real economic problems that enforcement of the Navigation Acts created for the British plantation owners and traders in the West Indies, Nelson was forced to navigate in those very dangerous political crosscurrents.

Regardless of the inherent political dangers, Nelson demonstrated his growing willingness to accept political risk to carry out his duty in terms of what he perceived as the largest objective involved. He described his dilemma in a letter to his friend Locker in March 1786: "I must either disobey my orders, or disobey Acts of Parliament. . . . I determined upon the former."[10] Much later in his career the same dilemma and approach were expressed in general terms and on a grander scale in a letter to the duke of Clarence (the former Prince William): "To serve my King, and to destroy the French, I consider as the great order of all, from which little ones spring; and if one of these little ones militate against it, (for who can tell exactly at a distance?) I go back to obey the great order and object."[11]

KING COMMERCE

By the mid-1780s there were very powerful economic factors bearing on Britain's attempts to fashion its sea-based strategy against France. The loss of the American colonies was among the most acutely negative of those factors. The loss of the burgeoning cities and farmlands as markets for British products was a serious, some claimed devastating, economic setback for Britain. Equally painful was the loss of the raw materials from the American colonies that were helping to fuel

Britain's economic growth. Among the most important goods were the naval raw materials, such as pine masts and spars, that had been supplied to the British Navy and merchant marine by the North American colonies.

Some people believed that the loss of the American colonies would be fatal to the British Empire; Lord Chatham, for example, had referred to those possessions as "the fountain of our wealth." But it soon became apparent that Britain's economic engine, fueled by her empire and protected by her maritime power, was powerful enough to continue driving the country's rise in both domestic economic growth and global power. A remarkable demonstration of this was the restoration of British exports to the United States after the Revolution. Within five years those exports grew to exceed 90 percent of their prewar value, and this important trade with the growing American market continued to rise steadily.

One consequence of the economic loss resulting from the American Revolution—and again a part of the political environment in which Nelson operated in the West Indies—was that Britain's political leadership looked to the nation's other overseas possessions to take up the economic slack. This meant that the need to maintain a viable economic base in the West Indies was in direct conflict with the overall need for Britain to maintain its global maritime power through such instruments as the Navigation Acts.

For Nelson, as he began his operations in the West Indies in 1784, the result was that he earned not only the immediate enmity of the local colonists but the long-term ill will of those in Britain who had economic interests in the West Indies. That group's pervasive influence in London could be measured by its powerful lobby there; some said it was the most powerful British lobby of the time. Those merchants and plantation owners would provide an ongoing source of negative influence in high places on Nelson's career. The situation added up to a special kind of double jeopardy for him.

In spite of the serious threats to his career that resulted from his decision to vigorously enforce the Navigation Acts, Nelson never wavered in his pursuit of that mission. One reason was that it was not a choice by chance. Rather, it was a choice driven by his ability to see beyond his immediate situation and grasp the larger strategic issues involved. Another, little-discussed factor was also in play at the time: Nelson was a strongly committed monarchist. His references to the American traders and those willing to deal with them as inimical to British interests were frequent and emotional enough to demonstrate that this was not a strictly intellectual question for him. Any British subject who served his or her own financial interests rather than obey the laws of the king was a rebel. And the Americans were the worst kind, for they had been successful. Nelson's emotional belief in the political and ethical virtues of the monarchical system of government was an important emotional component to his interpretation of his duty.

AN OVERRIDING FORCE

From the long perspective of history, perhaps the biggest single economic factor of the time was the accelerating force of the Industrial Revolution in Britain. Access to iron ore and coal, the means of capital accumulation and investment, internal communication over a functional system of roads and canals, the development of machines and techniques that sharply multiplied production rates, a strong agricultural base, population growth, and a tradition of foreign trade with a navy to protect it: all joined to form the critical mass for one of the major societal changes of modern history. The catalyst for that history-making takeoff of the Industrial Revolution in Britain clearly was the British population itself.

A spirit of enterprise and self-confidence made for a phenomenon that was greater than the sum of its commercial-industrial-military-political parts. That economic energy influenced events in general in *Boreas*'s operating area. Moreover, the young captain who walked her quarterdeck was, in a naval context, an embodiment of that national spirit. He was a man who clearly understood that maritime power meant a great deal more than a powerful navy. He was a naval officer with confidence in his nation, his navy, and his ship; he was a leader who took an active and unapologetic approach to his assignments. A. T. Mahan described him as "the one man who in himself summed up and embodied the greatness of the possibilities which Sea Power comprehends. . . . the personification of the Navy of Great Britain."[12] And in the West Indies Nelson was strongly driven by his awareness of those momentous "possibilities which Sea Power comprehends."

Six

Troubled Waters

Keep ye the law—be swift in all obedience.

—RUDYARD KIPLING

Nelson arrived in Barbados in June 1784; what he found in his new theater of operations surprised and troubled him. In January 1785, after only six months on the station, he wrote from Basseterre Roads in St. Christopher (generally called St. Kitts today) to Captain Locker about the state of things: "The longer I am on this Station the worse I like it. Our Commander . . . is led by the advice of the Islanders to admit the Yankees to a Trade; at least to wink at it. . . . I for one, am determined not to suffer the Yankees to come where my ship is. . . . They will first become the Carriers, and next have possession of our Islands, are we ever again embroiled in French war. The residents of these Islands are Americans by connexion and by interest, and are inimical to Great Britain."[1]

In addition to reflecting his understanding of the broader issues involved in the enforcement of the Navigation Acts, Nelson's words revealed not only a conviction that the new United States was to be added to Britain's enemies list, but a belief that the British West Indian colonists who were willing to participate in the trade with the United States were of a kind with Britain's former subjects to the north. His assessment of the British West Indian colonists was strikingly close to that of John Adams in America.

SAILING IN TROUBLED WATERS

It was a nasty state of affairs for Nelson, and it must have seemed as if the series of disagreeable events immediately following his appointment to command of _Boreas_ was beginning to extend into a pattern for his West Indies assignment. One of the worst aspects of his situation was that he could not count on the support of his immediate naval superior, of the British governor-general, or of the British plantation owners and merchants in the West Indies, almost all of whom either were actively involved in the illegal trade with the United States or passively condoned it. Yet Nelson, as second in command for the Navy and senior officer afloat, had major responsibilities that required the cooperation and support of the local military and civilian infrastructure, and the lack of that support was a serious handicap for him.

Those circumstances notwithstanding, in the middle of his complaint to his friend Locker he emphatically declared that, at least in the vicinity of his ship, the

Navigation Acts would vigorously be enforced. And Nelson's use of the words, "where my ship is," sharply illuminates his limited naval capability to consistently enforce a significant British policy in the important theater where he was operating.

The merchants and shipowners of the new United States, for their part, felt that they had a right to trade with anyone willing to do so, regardless of British maritime laws. And the colonists in the West Indies, as has been noted, were more than willing to participate in that trade. They believed that more than their prosperity was at stake; as they saw it, their economic survival depended on trade with the United States. In that environment American ship captains, many of whom were experienced in the North American–West Indian trade that had flourished before the American Revolution, vigorously renewed their former activities. As they did so, they used an array of ruses to skirt the Navigation Acts, not because they believed they actually were deceiving anyone—the local merchants had no doubts about the identity and circumstances of their trading partners—but to provide a measure of legal cover for their operations.

One of the favorite devices of the American captains was to feign a seagoing emergency. By declaring that their ship was in distress from storm or other damage and that there was mortal danger to the crew, they were able to appeal to an unwritten but universal law of the sea: namely, one must aid ships and seamen in distress, whatever their nationality. Once in port the American ships supposedly in distress would proceed to unload their cargos, at times "paying" for the repairs with the cargo they had off-loaded. They would then reload in the same port or move on to another port to take on northbound cargo under the same or a different pretext. They then would sail north to American East Coast ports and start the cycle over again.

COLLINGWOOD PRECIPITATES THE CONFLICT

Nelson's friend, Captain Cuthbert Collingwood of the frigate HMS *Mediator,* was involved in an incident with a ship practicing such tactics shortly after Nelson's arrival. In mid-December 1785 Collingwood was patrolling off St. John's, Antigua, when he encountered an American vessel making for the harbor. When queried, the American master claimed that he had a serious problem with his mainmast and intended to enter St. John's for repairs. Collingwood had the mast inspected by *Mediator*'s carpenter, who determined that the damage was not serious. Collingwood then ordered the American ship to anchor alongside *Mediator* in St. John's Harbour and proceeded to have his own ship's carpenter carry out the repairs. At the first opportunity the master of the American ship went ashore, where he complained to the governor of the Leeward Islands, General Sir Thomas Shirley.

Shirley first sought the advice of the local king's counsel, and then that of the attorney general of Grenada, who was in Antigua at the time. The counsel opined: "I have always apprehended that the coercion for an obedience to the Laws of Trade, Navigation or the Revenue is peculiarly committed to the Board of Customs, and to the subordinate officers of the Customs. . . . Any military interference without requisition from these officers of the Customs in any port of the British Dominions is certainly very unusual and singular."[3]

With the opinion of the king's counsel and the attorney general in hand, Shirley then wrote to the British secretary of state in London about the incident. In the letter to London Shirley identified Collingwood's action as "a circumstance which has given much dissatisfaction," and asked the secretary of state, in true bureaucratic style, for a "plan" to resolve the dispute.

A few days after the incident Shirley also wrote to Admiral Hughes questioning what Collingwood had done, complaining that those actions had closed the port of St. John's. He also questioned Collingwood's authority to detain the American ship. In the letter to Hughes, Shirley described Captain Collingwood's action as a "circumstance which has lately given rise to much disquiet and dissatisfaction to the Inhabitants of this Colony." It appears that Governor Shirley was receiving angry pressure from the local plantation owners and merchants. He apparently was being driven by public opinion rather than by a consideration of the basic issues involved.

NELSON ENTERS THE FRAY

In essence, Governor Shirley and his legal advisers were challenging not just the legality of Collingwood's specific action, but in broader terms, the Navy's legal authority to take the initiative with aggressive action against the direct trade between America and the British West Indies colonies. The battle lines were being drawn between civilian and naval military authority, a recurring conflict between diplomatic and military points of view that continues within many governments to present times. In another context, Nelson also was confronting the overall issue of civilian control of the military, a concept that has continued to evolve, particularly among Western nations, to the present.

Nelson quickly entered the conflict, and in the testy exchange of correspondence that ensued, he took on not only Governor-General Shirley and his legal advisers, but his own military commander, Admiral Hughes, as well. His challenge to Governor Shirley lacked any hint of conciliation or deference. In January 1785 he wrote to him: "I conceive it the duty of all Governors, officers of the Navy, in short all officers under the Crown to suppress illicit trade, and to take care that the Laws which the Wisdom of our Parliments has made be not evaded, either by Oaths, Protests or Otherwise."[3]

Nelson went on in the same letter to frame the developing dispute between himself and the local civilian and military leadership around the basic question of civilian versus military authority: "The Wisdom of our Legislature has directed the Act of Navigation to Admirals and Captains of the Navy well knowing that those whose profession is the sea must be the best judges of the accidents which may happen upon that element." Nelson's lecture to Shirley continued with references to civilian-military protocol, and ended with a thinly disguised threat: "I have . . . transmitted Home such accounts relative to the Trade and Navigation of these Colonies as I have thought fit, and shall from time to time continue that practice whenever it is necessary." The defiance in the tone of this statement is unmistakable, but arguably the most surprising thing about this letter is not its audacious tone, bordering on contempt, but the skill with which Nelson marshaled his arguments and then accurately aimed his verbal shots at his opponents' vulnerabilities.

Also in January 1785 Nelson wrote an even more astonishing letter to his commander-in-chief, Admiral Hughes, a man who could break him. His tone was not one bit more conciliatory than in his correspondence with Governor-General Shirley. Again he focused on the issue of the Navy's authority: "No person can know better than Sea Officers of which I shall inform the Governors, etc: when they acquaint me for what reason they have countenanced the admission of

Foreigners." Later in the same letter he added: "The Governors may be imposed upon by false declarations; we, who are on the spot, cannot."[4]

Nelson's point that the naval commander on the spot was in a better position to make decisions than off-site civilian officials, or even off-site naval officers, was one that would be repeated later in his career. One notable instance came in 1799, when his immediate superior, Admiral Lord Keith, ordered him to leave Naples and the Kingdom of the Two Sicilies. Nelson refused, claiming that he knew the importance of protecting that particular British ally because he was on the scene in Naples where the Sicilian court was located. As was the case in the Caribbean, Nelson's decision to ignore an order caused him serious problems at the Admiralty.

OTHER MEANS OF SKIRTING THE LAW

One of the worst aspects of the situation from Nelson's point of view was the complicity of the local customs officials. Nelson was particularly harsh in his judgment of those individuals because he correctly observed that they were sworn to uphold British law, not to interpret it. Nelson went so far as to suggest that for them it was not a matter of preserving their livelihoods, but simple corruption. In January 1785, in one of his contentious letters to Governor Shirley, he wrote: "Since I have been appointed to the Station among these islands, I know that several Americans have received Permits from the Custom House here to sell their Cargoes, and these Permits obtained upon very frivolous pretexts."[5] Later, in a petition to the king, he referred to how "[t]he Custom House seemed to glory in the ruin they were heaping upon Great Britain and seemed to think they were beyond the reach of power."[6] In the same petition he noted how "the Custom House laughed" at his presumption to take action against the American trade, threatening him that he certainly would be sued if he did so.

Another subterfuge of the American captains involved a temporary change in the registry of their ships. One of the most common ruses was to temporarily convert an American vessel to Spanish registry in order to operate under trading rights in the British colonies granted by a 1763 British order of the Treasury. Before calling at a British West Indies port, the American ships would call at an island held by the Spanish, and there they would secure official papers identifying them as Spanish ships involved in local interisland trade. Nelson described the practice in his dispatches and correspondence on several occasions. In one letter to the Admiralty in August 1786, he concluded: "I have but little doubt, although their decks are loaded with cattle, that in their holds they bring American produce."[7]

SELECTIVE VISION

In the same letter to the Admiralty, Nelson, as on other occasions, showed his grasp of the larger issues involved in the illegal trade, beyond enforcing the law for its own sake. "I have seized one of these American Spaniards. . . . This traffic, I must take the liberty of observing, brings to the King of Spain a considerable revenue; it will increase the Ship-building of America, and raise the numbers of her Seamen, while, on the contrary, it will decrease the British Shipping and Seamen in these Islands. These Americans will take off our rum, and carry it to America, so that our vessels will shortly have no trade to those States. They will be again the Carriers between these Islands and America."[8]

But although Nelson understood and supported the underlying premise for the Navigation Acts, his analysis of the situation lacked any recognition of the counterargument about the strategic importance to Britain of maintaining economically productive colonies in the West Indies, colonies whose economic viability had been seriously damaged during the American Revolution. Further, he showed no willingness to recognize the plight of the colonists themselves, many of whom feared for their financial survival because of the region's economic instability and even for their lives because of the significant and growing imbalance of numbers between the British colonists and their slaves. In some instances the slaves outnumbered the colonists by as much as twenty to one, and slave rebellions among the islands were not unknown.

Despite his single-minded determination, however, it became clear over time that with an insufficient number of British ships permanently assigned in the West Indies, there were serious limits to Nelson's ability to do more than slow down the illegal trade. Nevertheless, he tried mightily, and as a result he was ostracized by many of the islands' merchants and landowners. Eventually he faced a legal threat that could have thrown him into unmanageable debt and ended his career.

NO ANCHOR TO WINDWARD

A hard-charging young naval captain should be able to pursue his duty with the knowledge that he can take risks without unduly putting his career in danger, and the unwavering support of his immediate military senior would be crucial in that regard. Unfortunately, as the captain of *Boreas*, senior officer afloat, and second in naval command on the West Indies Station, Nelson lacked that "anchor to windward." In

October 1784 in a letter to Captain Locker, Nelson labeled his military commander, Admiral Hughes, as "tolerable." A month later, in another letter to Locker, he was much more cutting: "The Admiral and all about him are great ninnies." Later, in May 1785, in a letter to his brother William, Nelson got to the heart of the matter: "[O]ur Admiral does not support us. He is an _excellent fiddler._" Then by March 1786 he adopted a mocking tone in yet another letter to Captain Locker: "Sir Richard Hughes . . . is a fiddler; therefore, as his time is taken up tuning that instrument, you will consequently expect the Squadron is cursedly out of tune."[9]

A second area of potential support that was, in fact, lacking involved the local customs officials. Particularly in his correspondence with the Admiralty, Nelson was bitter in his condemnation of their inaction in the face of what clearly was, by British law, illegal trade. In a "Memorial to the King" in June 1785 on the subject of that trade, Nelson was pointed: "[Y]our Majesty's proclamation prohibiting all Trade with America, to and from the West Indies, (except in British bottoms, owned and navigated by the people of your Majesty's Dominions and Territories,) was most shamefully evaded by colouring American vessels with British Registers, by which means . . . and connivance of others of the Officers of His Majesty's Customs in the West India Islands nearly the whole Trade between America and your Majesty's said Colonies was carried on in American bottoms."[10]

Finally, there was the lack of support from the local population in general, and this had an impact on Nelson in a special way. It heightened the sense of isolation for him while deployed on a foreign station. Normally a naval captain's fellow countrymen among the communities in an overseas theater of operations would be a most welcome

and important support system. But because he was perceived as a threat to the livelihoods of the local British
colonists, who were struggling to recover from the near economic ruin of the American Revolution, the situation was
reversed for Nelson. The local plantation owners, merchants, and officials displayed open animosity toward him
(though there were some notable exceptions). Eventually
they launched legal suits against him and threatened to have
him arrested if he stepped ashore. Thus, in many places and
for extended periods of time, Nelson was a virtual prisoner
in his own ship. At one stage he pointed out in a narrative
probably sent to Prince William Henry: "Seven weeks I was
kept a close prisoner to my Ship; nor did I ever learn that
the Admiral took any steps for my release."[11] That unmistakable lack of support from his immediate naval superior
would have been particularly distressing for a dedicated and
proactive young captain.

In an interesting side note, the severely adversarial relations with the local populace in the West Indies during
Nelson's *Boreas* command contrasted sharply with the phe-
nomenal popular support for him in Britain that began
building later in his career, particularly after his brilliant and
courageous contribution to the British victory at the Battle
of Cape St. Vincent in 1797. That popular support was to swell
steadily, and upon his departure from England in September
1805 to fight his last battle for his king and country, he left to
the cheers of a crowd lining the shoreline. Marking his understanding of the true character of that support, Nelson turned
to his flag captain, Sir Thomas Hardy, and remarked: "I had
their huzzas before—I have their hearts now."[12]

In the West Indies between 1784 and 1787, however, the
importance of public support was vividly demonstrated to
Nelson in a negative context. And that surely made him more

appreciative of the unparalleled popular support he received later in his career.

Nelson's difficulties with Admiral Hughes probably were somewhat mitigated by Lady Hughes. Despite Nelson's unflattering comments about her and her "infernal clack," it is apparent that Lady Hughes formed a favorable opinion of the young captain during her voyage in *Boreas* from England to the West Indies. It seems that she had the common sense and basic good nature to accept that Nelson had no interest in her daughter. Convincing evidence of her positive opinion of Nelson is found in comments that she made in correspondence to a friend, George Matcham, in 1806. In particular, she had been impressed by his attention to "the young gentlemen who had the happiness of being on his Quarter-Deck."[13]

In her letter to Matcham, Lady Hughes admitted that she was not qualified to assess Nelson's professional capabilities, and concentrated on how he helped the more timid of the midshipmen to conquer their fear of working aloft. She also noted his way of encouraging them in their duties and his habit of taking them, in ones and twos, to the social events to which he was invited. Lady Hughes's favorable opinion, working unofficially but powerfully on a day-to-day basis, certainly made Admiral Hughes more tolerant of Nelson's challenging aggressiveness than he would have been otherwise. It was a phenomenon recognizable to any officer who understands the potential influence of an admiral's spouse.

A notable exception to the adversarial relationship Nelson had with Britain's West Indian populace, and a second area of support for Nelson, was John Herbert, president of Nevis. As the influential owner of a major plantation on the island and the head of one of the island's most respected families, Herbert had much to lose by Nelson's active enforcement of the Navigation Acts. However, he obviously liked and respected Nelson, and to his credit even offered to post bond for him if he were arrested, saying that "the captain had done no more than his duty, though he was one of the greatest sufferers by it."[14]

In addition, Herbert invited Nelson to his home, Montpelier. The dwelling, at the time the largest on the island, was part of Herbert's Nevis plantation estate; it was set high on a hillside, where there would almost always be a cooling ocean breeze. Considering the attitude toward Nelson among Herbert's peers and the lack of comfort in the close quarters of his ship, Montpelier, which Nelson initially visited in 1784, must have seemed like heaven to him. In time the idyllic site high on the Nevis hillside would take on even greater significance, for it was there that Nelson met his wife-to-be, Frances Nisbet, who was Herbert's niece and the social organizer and hostess for her uncle at Montpelier.

EMERGING LEADERSHIP QUALITIES

The adversities that Nelson faced in the West Indies, including physical and social isolation and the lack of official civilian and naval support for his actions, would have forced an accommodation from many, perhaps most, officers in his situation. For Nelson, it produced the reverse; it tempered and sharpened the cutting edge of his basic leadership qualities. It was a period that dramatically brought forth his willingness to define his duty himself and to pursue that duty aggressively, even at the risk of losing his career and suffering social sanctions in the process.

Significantly this tempering and sharpening process was taking place in a noncombat environment. The pressures and threats did not come accompanied by the excitement of battle. And in sharp contrast to the compact violence of combat, they were drawn out over a long period of time, when fatigue, discouragement, self-doubt, and boredom could wear down even strong resolve. In time the full array of leadership qualities that Nelson was developing in the West Indies, and that would have to sustain him during the relatively long gaps between the frenzied action of his great battles, were just as important in his character as the more attention-getting qualities he needed in combat.

DEFINING DUTY UNDER PRESSURE

Nelson's developing attitudes about duty were severely tested in the hostile environment of the West Indies. Under the intense pressure of the circumstances, duty increasingly was becoming something that he constructed within himself, not something that was imposed externally by orders or regulations. Also at this time he was beginning to define his duty in terms of two factors: the larger objectives involved and the immediate circumstances.

The confrontations in the West Indies with his immediate naval commander, the governor-general, customs officials, and the merchants and plantation owners of the islands tested this intensely internal approach to his duty. As a result of this process Nelson's tour in the West Indies in *Boreas* was not only a time of conflict-laden events, it was a forerunner of similar and even more challenging events as his career developed and his fame grew. Despite the immediate, short-term negative results of his actions after he returned to

England, in the longer term his internalized approach to duty, as professionally risky as it was, became a permanent and highly visible part of his character.

WRITTEN EVIDENCE

The strongest indications that the subject of duty was continuously on Nelson's mind in the West Indies appear in the form of the frequent references to the subject in his correspondence. These references are found in dispatches to the Admiralty and in correspondence with his friends; they even were included in letters of endearment to his future wife. In the latter instances they often took the form of brief lectures to Fanny, such as a portion of a letter written in May 1786: "Duty is the great business of a Sea-officer. All private considerations must give way to it, however painful it is."[15]

That no doubt sincere statement about a naval officer's duty was, in hindsight, one of the clearest predictors of the marital troubles to come for the couple. And if the statements about duty today seem stiff-necked and overblown coming from a young frigate captain, they were clearly nothing of the kind when considered in the light of the totality of Nelson's career.

One of the most thought-provoking features of these early statements by Nelson about duty, particularly those that relate to the Navigation Acts, is their unequivocal character. There were no musings about whether or not he might be right, no doubts about his actions, and no doubts about his authority. And there certainly was nothing apologetic or even tentative about the defense of his actions to his immediate naval senior or the Admiralty.

Just how strongly Nelson felt on this subject emerges from the words he wrote in a message to Admiral Hughes in January 1785. In this relatively long letter to his commander, he stated: "[A]t a time when Great Britain is using every endeavour to suppress illicit Trade at Home, it is not wished that the ships upon this Station should be singular, by being the only spectators of the illegal Trade which I know is carried on at these Islands. The Governor may be imposed upon by false declarations; we, who are on the spot, cannot."[16]

The unvarnished language Nelson used in his arguments with Admiral Hughes and Governor Shirley stands in sharp contrast with their more tentative letters. Both men seemed to be groping for arguments that would protect them if their actions were found to be wrong in the eyes of the Admiralty; they were political in their approach. Nelson, however, reflected only the unshakable conviction that his actions were consistent with the law and the greater interests of his country. And Nelson was not merely venting his frustration in his aggressive tone; he was putting those with whom he was in opposition on notice that there was risk for them in the dispute as well.

Nelson's letter of January 1785 to Admiral Hughes was a bold statement—bordering on impertinent—to his military commander, more like the tone that would be used by a senior officer to one considerably junior. And viewed in the context of his letter at the same time to Governor Shirley, it was amazingly risky for an officer who was yet to reach thirty years of age to lecture a senior official with a distinguished army career, who also was twice his age. It was the kind of tone that infuriated many of the senior officers in the British Navy, as well as the civilian leadership at the Admiralty, during his brilliant career. And it no doubt created significant areas of resentment that would affect his career immediately after his tour in the West Indies. But Nelson's willingness to deal bluntly with his seniors and accept the consequences also made him a uniquely valuable naval leader in time of war, one who would just as fearlessly tell the truth to his seniors as he would face the guns of his enemies in battle.

Seven

Legal Morass

If laws are their enemies, they will be enemies to laws.

——EDMUND BURKE

As events developed in the West Indies, Nelson had much more serious matters to contend with than the ill will of the local populace. His Navy career and financial viability would soon be threatened by a series of legal actions by irate colonists.

As the dispute over Nelson's actions in connection with the Navigation Acts moved into a legal phase, it appeared as if Nelson would be "outgunned" by his opponents. Without a doubt he was outnumbered, since he was contending with the governor-general, the governor's legal advisers, and an array of local residents. In addition, he was, at least initially, actively opposed by his own military commander. His opponents quickly armed themselves with opinions from the local legal officials, opinions that supported their hands-off approach to the trade in question and cast doubt on the legality of direct action against the trade by Navy ship captains. They also made it clear that, with few exceptions, Nelson would not be welcome at the homes of the more influential members of the various islands' communities.

In response, Nelson applied elements of his future combat doctrine to his legal conflict with the civilian officials and plantation owners. He began by seizing the initiative; then he fought aggressively to the finish. And that developing Nelsonian doctrine served him just as well in the legal arena in the West Indies as it did in later combat situations in the Mediterranean, Baltic, and Atlantic. It enabled him eventually to win the court battle over the Navigation Acts, when the odds appeared to be heavily against him.

DEALING FROM KNOWLEDGE

One of the important weapons that Nelson had in his conflict over the Navigation Acts was his specific knowledge of the laws in question. It is clear that he had studied the acts before embarking on his efforts to stop the U.S.–West Indies trade, and he supplemented his layman's knowledge with legal opinions from others, whenever reliable legal counsel was available to him. From the outset, he based his primary arguments first on knowledge of the laws and then on the direct connection of those laws with Britain's maritime power and overall economic viability. It was a two-pronged strategy that enabled him eventually to carry the day.

It also was an early example of the crystal-clear thinking so characteristic of Nelson's leadership, something that went well beyond charisma and the adrenaline-driven reactions to combat. Nearly two hundred years later, then–U.S. president John Kennedy reminded us in succinct terms of the critical linkage that Nelson instinctively understood and used: "Leadership and learning are indispensable to each other."[1]

One of the most telling examples of how Nelson used his specific knowledge of the acts came early in the difficult confrontation with Admiral Hughes. In January 1785 Nelson wrote to Hughes to discuss, among other things, the admiral's order that the British naval officers on the station were merely to detain ships suspected of illegal trade and "on no account to hinder, or prevent such Foreign ship or vessel from going in accordingly, or to interfere any further in her subsequent proceedings" unless approved by the governor-general.[2] Hughes's order effectively reduced the role of Nelson and the other British Navy captains on the station to that of monitors, rather than proactive enforcers of the law.

However, the actual language of the acts was unequivocal in its reference to the role of the British Navy captains. The specific wording was that all foreign ships trading in the West Indies were subject to "forfeiture of ship and cargo; and all admirals and commanders of the King's ships are authorized to make seizure of ships offending herein."[3] The law thus spoke clearly on the positive authority of captains to seize ships violating the acts. Nelson was on firm legal ground, and he knew it. Of greatest importance, Nelson was willing to take action based on his conviction of what was the right thing to do, despite the personal risks to his future that were involved.

In his argument to Hughes against placing the final authority on matters involving the enforcement of the Navigation Acts with the local political and customs officials, Nelson directly challenged the admiral's order. In blunt terms, he said that he would never cooperate with a local official in circumventing the law, which is what Nelson contended those officials consistently were doing. His words were unequivocal: "Whilst I have the honour to command an English Man of War, I never shall allow myself to be subservient to the will of any Governor, nor co-operate with him in doing illegal acts. Presidents of Council I feel myself superior to. They shall make proper application to me for whatever they may want to come by water."[4] In a very real sense, Nelson had chosen a general approach to the dispute, a doctrine that later he would articulate for combat: "The boldest measures are the safest."[5]

Nelson didn't stop with the points of law, he also argued the importance of strict enforcement of the acts to Britain's basic economic survival. He even used an argument that ran through his later justifications for departing from orders: he was the man on the scene and the one who could easily tell who was falsely swearing "through a nine inch plank," while officials ashore could be and regularly were easily deceived by the American ship captains. In reality, of course, it was more a matter of the officials going along with a masquerade than failing to perceive a deception.

But it was toward the end of his letter to his commander that he fired his most devastating verbal broadside with a blunt declaration: "I know the Navigation Laws."[6] There was no mistaking the determination to continue his course of action, even if it put his career at risk. Of greater significance, Nelson made it clear to Hughes that there was considerable risk for him as well if he supported the hands-off approach to the illegal trade. Clearly, Nelson's statement about knowing the law was much more than bluster; it was a sound psychological tactic to get his opponent off balance. It also suggests that he was acting on an assessment of his opponent—in this instance, that he was dealing with an officer who was irresolute and who was not willing to study the actual laws involved in the dispute. Again the parallels with his later approach to combat are noteworthy.

At one point, when Hughes admitted that he was not familiar with the law and had never actually read the Navigation Acts, Nelson aggressively pressed his initiative; he personally carried a copy of the acts to the admiral. To strengthen the impact of his action, he did so in the company of a witness, Captain Cuthbert Collingwood. For good measure, Nelson pointed out that it was his understanding that copies of the Navigation Acts were provided to all British naval officers.

By his own admission, Hughes had based his order on what he termed the "good advice" of others, rather than on firsthand knowledge of the laws in question. That admission gave Nelson the opportunity to take the initiative in the disagreement with his commander squarely into his own hands, and he seized it quickly by noting that the acts established that the captains of the ships in the West Indies were to "proceed against all attempts of illicit Trade by the Americans."[7]

Although Hughes never consistently and publicly supported the authority of his second in command to the degree he should have, Nelson had created enough legal maneuvering room to pursue his own interpretation of the acts. If Nelson could not secure the full support of his admiral, he at least had neutralized him in the conflict; Nelson could now focus more efficiently on the other parts of his legal battle. This aspect of the struggle over the Navigation Acts offers a fascinating example of Nelson's mental agility, bold tactics, and ability to accurately assess a situation—qualities that he later applied to more physically dangerous and more geopolitically important circumstances in his major battles.

THE ONGOING LEGAL BATTLE

One of the first legal maneuvers of the local merchants and plantation owners was to seek a royal exemption from the

Navigation Acts for the West Indies. In one of his strongest letters to Admiral Hughes, written in January 1785, Nelson refers to that petition to the king and notes how the king had responded by saying that he "firmly believed and hoped that all his orders which were received by his Governors would be strictly obeyed."[8] That royal statement reinforced the previous action of the government commission that had refused to make any special trading allowances for the West Indies colonies, and Nelson used his knowledge of the circumstances to further strengthen his hand in pursuing his duty as he interpreted it.

An early legal showdown came in the spring of 1785, when Nelson seized first one and then four additional American ships at Nevis. The captains of the latter four ships, after they were interviewed by Nelson aboard *Boreas,* accused him of assault and illegal imprisonment. The accusation was based on the presence of an armed marine guard in the vicinity of the interview, a circumstance that would have been a part of the normal ship's routine rather than an attempt to intimidate the American captains. The American captains proceeded to secure writs for Nelson's arrest from local courts; in their action, the four captains claimed £4,000 in damages. An award by the court of those potential damages would have severely strained Nelson's finances; he himself described the amount as "an enormous sum." The importance of this financial threat to Nelson should not be underestimated. It was not a matter of potential financial inconvenience for him, but rather a prospect of financial ruin.

Nelson did appear at the two-day trial, and during the proceedings the court protected him from vigorous attempts by the complaining American captains to have him arrested. He played a strong role in his own defense and was cleared of the accusations by the judge. After the trial Nelson complained bitterly about being held "captive" in his own ship before the court proceedings by those who opposed his enforcement of the Navigation Acts. In describing the event later, however, Nelson also acknowledged the assistance of a good lawyer and the surprising support of John Herbert, president of Nevis. Herbert went so far as to offer to post bond up to £10,000 if Nelson was arrested when he appeared at court.[9]

The seizures of American ships attempting to directly trade in the West Indies, and the resulting legal battles, continued throughout the islands over the following several years of Nelson's tour. In February 1787 Nelson lamented to Captain Locker: "Since August . . . the Admiralty have not wrote me a single line, only to take the *Pegasus* and *Solebay* under my command. Many things have happened, and they have not either approved, nor otherwise, of my conduct."[10] He also complained of the difficulty of securing adequate legal representation to defend his seizures. There is no doubt that Nelson believed he had carried out his duty in spite of, rather than with the support of, his senior naval leadership in London or his local naval leadership in the West Indies.

It is clear that during the entire span of his time in *Boreas* in the West Indies, Nelson pursued his controversial enforcement of the Navigation Acts with limited official support, and at times even faced official opposition from more than one source. It is equally clear, however, that his exceptionally strong will and agile mind were enough to sustain his pursuit of his duty. And that irresistible determination was a quality that carried through to the very end of his career—through the physically and mentally stressful search for French admiral Pierre Villeneuve in the Mediterranean, Atlantic, and the West Indies, and the eventual destruction of the French-Spanish Combined Fleet at Cape Trafalgar in 1805. In both the dispute in the West Indies and the prelude to the Battle of Trafalgar, Nelson's dogged determination was a prerequisite to the eventual outcome. In the former instance, the result was a legal victory; in the latter situation, it was a combat victory that influenced the course of history by preventing the invasion of Britain and blunting Napoleon's military power.

THE LONG AND THE SHORT OF IT

In the short term, and on an unofficial but important basis, Nelson's legal battles in the West Indies did his career more harm than good. The enemies he made among the planters, merchants, and customs agents no doubt communicated their strong feelings to influential friends and relatives back in Britain. It is unlikely that Admiral Hughes spoke kindly of his second in command's performance of duty in the West Indies. In one of the ironies of Nelson's legal battles in the West Indies over the Navigation Acts, it was Admiral Hughes who actually was commended by the Admiralty for diligence in the protection of Britain's trade in the Caribbean. In a narrative that was probably written around June 1786 and sent to Prince William Henry, Nelson expressed "surprise that the Commander-in-Chief should be thanked for an act which he did not order, but which . . . by his order of the 29th December 1784, he ordered not to be."[11]

Further along in the report Nelson, in an understandable overstatement, describes how he "stood singly" in the active enforcement of the Navigation Acts. The propensity of a home-based, politically oriented military leadership to reward the guilty and punish the innocent was a frustration that Nelson, who was not a risk-averse commander, was learning to bear. However, he had to overcome that frustration and any negative residual impact on his attitude about his career in order to move on professionally. Nelson was learning that in the British Navy of his time, as in almost all other institutions over time, life is not always fair. It was an essential point for him to understand as he moved toward great military victories. And by the time the war with France was renewed in 1793, he had done just that.

But if there were negative short-term results of his tour in the West Indies, in the long run there also were important counterbalancing benefits for Nelson associated with his legal struggles there. Arguably the most important was the eventual reinforcement of his willingness to risk his career in carrying out his duty *as he saw it.* Even if his on-scene commander was less than supportive—at one point Nelson believed that Hughes was going to relieve him of his command—and even if his tour was largely unpleasant and stressful, in the end the Admiralty officially supported Nelson's vigorous enforcement of the Navigation Acts. It was the first major test of his political courage, and the eventual official approval of his actions, muted though it was, had to influence his willingness to risk his career in the future.

A FOCUS ON LEADERSHIP

A.T. Mahan provided one of the more interesting analyses of Nelson's legal battles over his aggressive enforcement of the Navigation Acts. As both a senior naval officer and a renowned naval analyst, Mahan extended the significance of Nelson's actions to halt the illegal trade in the West Indies to broad aspects of naval leadership, including combat. In his *Life of Nelson,* Mahan recognized the emotional dilemma involved for Nelson as well as the qualities of character that were illuminated in the situation: "This struggle with Sir Richard Hughes, in which Nelson took the undesirable, and to a naval officer invidious, step of disobeying orders, showed clearly, not only the loftiness of his motives, but the distinguishing features which constituted the strength of his character, both personal and military. There was an acute perception of the right thing to do, an entire readiness to assume all the responsibility of doing it, and above all an accurate judgment of the best way to do it,—to act with impunity to himself and with the most chances of success to his cause. Its analogy to a military situation is striking."[12]

Mahan went on to point out that there also was a wrong to be righted and risks to be taken in the process. In his view, if there was a weak point in Nelson's tactics in enforcing the Navigation Acts, it was a lack of sensitivity toward the senior naval officers and civilian officials involved, suggesting that "he betrayed some of the carelessness of sensibilities which the inexperience of youth is too apt to show towards age." But with due respect to Mahan, one has to wonder if a more tactful approach would have succeeded as well as Nelson's more abrasive approach.

Mahan concluded his analysis of the controversy over enforcement of the Navigation Acts: "(B)ut, upon a careful review of the whole, it appears . . . that his general course of action was distinctly right, judged by the standards of the time and the well-settled principles of military obedience, and that he pursued an extremely difficult line of conduct with singular resolution, with sound judgment, and, in the main, with an unusual amount of tact, without which he could scarcely have failed, however well purposing, to lay himself open to serious consequences. Certainly he achieved success."[13] This last point by Mahan goes to the heart of Nelson's public popularity and his ability to survive repeated "scrapes" with the Admiralty; he was a winner when it counted most.

Perhaps the most important point of Mahan's analysis is its focus on a personal quality of Nelson's, his resolution in adversity, even when confronted with potential career damage. And in analyzing this noncombat situation in Nelson's early career, Mahan illuminated one of the most important hallmarks of Nelson's later combat career, the ability to establish a winning doctrine. The situation was an important lesson for Nelson: doing the right thing was worth the risk. That lesson would help him to get past other political and bureaucratic inequities later in his career.

A DISAPPOINTING RETURN

When Nelson returned to Portsmouth, he immediately began receiving letters from the Admiralty admonishing him for detouring *Pegasus* to Jamaica, when the ship had been ordered to Nova Scotia. The Admiralty also reproved him for sending *Rattler* to Jamaica, again without securing orders from the Admiralty. There were, in addition, criticisms for perceived administrative errors, including his pardon and discharge of a seaman convicted of desertion. Certainly one of the most galling items was the Admiralty's refusal to confirm Nelson's appointment of a new commanding officer of *Rattler,* whose captain, Wilfred Collingwood, brother of Nelson's friend Cuthbert Collingwood, had died in May 1787 while all three men were assigned to the West Indies Station. That refusal seemed to epitomize the predominant pettiness of the Admiralty's assessment of Nelson's efforts in the West Indies between 1784 and 1787.

Nelson had to be both surprised and depressed by the deluge of official and informal rebukes that greeted him. He would have been surprised because he had handled his overall assignment in the West Indies with perseverance and political courage. He would have been depressed because the official criticisms, no matter how petty, did not augur well for his securing another command. As Nelson sat in *Boreas*'s cabin in Portsmouth in August 1787, writing to his friends and complaining of a sore throat and general ill health triggered by the rain and cold, he may well have thought back to the troublesome beginning of his deployment in Boreas and the many bad omens that preceded his departure.

Eight

The Schomberg Affair

[R]equire nothing that is unreasonable of your officers . . . but see
that whatever is required be punctually complied with.

—GENERAL GEORGE WASHINGTON

saac Schomberg was first lieutenant aboard HMS *Pegasus,* the ship commanded by twenty-two-year-old Prince William Henry. In clear terms, Schomberg was placed in his position to manage the safety of a ship and crew commanded by a royal captain with limited experience as a naval officer and with—as one Nelson biographer described the prince's personality—"the temperament of a martinet and the manners of a bully."[1] Schomberg was a very competent seaman and a stubborn officer with a Hanoverian family background. Like some other officers in *Pegasus,* he had little professional respect for the prince. Not surprisingly, he clashed with his royal captain, who managed to emphasize his own lack of experience with petty orders for his officers and crew.

NELSON IN THE MIDDLE

When *Pegasus* and Prince William arrived in the West Indies in November 1786, Nelson automatically became his immediate naval senior. Yet as a member of royalty, the prince was owed deference by anyone below him in the royal order. That certainly included Nelson, a commoner by birth and unmistakably an outsider to the royal-by-blood circle. Just as significant, Nelson perceived the prince as a potentially positive influence on his naval career. Given Nelson's propensity for angering his seniors at the Admiralty, the latter was particularly important.

Nelson's position with regard to the prince was a difficult one for any British naval officer, particularly one with a strong sense of duty and a protective attitude about his own authority. On face value, working closely with the prince was an opportunity to gain influence at the Admiralty, Whitehall, and court. It was also a chance to secure that influence for well into the future, since William was in line to assume the throne, which he eventually did, as William IV. But the threat embedded in the situation was at least equal to the opportunity. If his reporting senior earned the displeasure of William, the officer might, for all practical purposes, see his naval career brought to an end. The threatening half of the equation was particularly acute in the light of William's personality; he was a heavy-drinking womanizer who at times focused more strongly on the privileges of his birth than on the responsibilities associated with his naval rank and his position as captain of a warship.

Nelson's relationship with the prince involved an additional factor, something beyond royal precedence and career ambition: this was Nelson's deep emotional commitment to the monarchical system of government. That commitment was, in turn, tightly interwoven with his patriotism and even his very strong, Christian religious beliefs. Nelson unequivocally was a monarchist, and in the coming years his loyalty to the monarchical system was to be intensified in his role as a senior naval commander in deadly combat against revolutionary and Napoleonic France. On more than one occasion he wrote of his particular hatred of republicanism and the excesses that followed the French Revolution. The British monarchy was, for Nelson, a bulwark against those republican excesses, and William, his character shortcomings notwithstanding, was a piece of the sociopolitical rampart that the British monarchy represented for Nelson.

AN EXPLOSIVE SITUATION

The problem between Prince William Henry and Lieutenant Schomberg became apparent to Nelson when he first went aboard *Pegagsus* in late 1786. On that occasion there was an unseemly exchange between the lieutenant and his captain over what the appropriate dress of the ship's company should be. A public exchange such as this between a captain and his first lieutenant, particularly on the ship's quarterdeck, was an egregious breach of good order and discipline on the part of both parties. The unusual situation was noted by Nelson, who later wrote: "The manner in which this was spoke made a much greater impression upon me than all that happened afterwards for I plainly saw all was not right."[2]

What came next could hardly have been a surprise to anyone. The discord between William and his first lieutenant once again came to the surface, and once again it was on the quarterdeck of their ship. The issue for the prince was that Schomberg and a junior officer had dispatched one of the ship's boats without notifying him. Under normal circumstances, if Schomberg's action was a departure from the captain's standing orders, the event arguably should have been the subject of a private discussion between the captain and the first lieutenant. This would be true particularly if the discussion involved an admonishment on the part of the captain.

But the circumstances definitely were not normal, and the prince cited Schomberg in the ship's general order book for neglect of duty. The incident, once made a part of the ship's official records, could very likely have had a significantly adverse effect on Schomberg's career. His recourses were to accept the official, career-threatening admonishment or to request a court-martial to vindicate his behavior and clear his professional reputation. Although he risked an additional, even more significant scar on his personal Navy record, Schomberg chose the latter course. His decision can be explained by what appeared to be a justifiable belief in his professional abilities and the correctness of his own conduct. In his request for a court-martial he stated that he was accused of "neglect of duty . . . of which I do not conceive myself guilty."[3]

As an additional factor in the situation, it appeared that there were other officers in *Pegasus* who were close to requesting courts-martial for reasons similar to Schomberg's. Nelson, as the senior naval officer afloat on the station, was the one required to act upon Schomberg's request. Perhaps fortunately for all three of the principals in the dispute, there was not a sufficient number of senior officers in the West Indies to convene a legal court-martial. In that circumstance Nelson had some, but not much, maneuvering room.

NELSON TAKES ACTION

Nelson's decision was to place Schomberg under arrest. Although on face value it could be said that he was taking the side of the prince and in the process protecting his own

career, it was a sensible move. There would be no further routine contact between the two protagonists, and the arrest gave
Nelson a brief amount of time to try to calm the situation
down. One of his first actions was to write, on 23 January
1787, to William: "I have the honour of acquainting your
Royal Highness that in consequence of a letter which I have
this day received from Lieutenant Isaac Schomberg, first
Lieutenant of His Majesty's Ship *Pegasus,* under your command, I have thought proper to order him under Arrest, and
beg you will grant him such indulgences, or lay such restric-
tions on him, during his Arrest, as his behaviour shall appear
to you to deserve."[4] One of the biggest problems with Nelson's
placing Schomberg under arrest was that Schomberg remained aboard *Pegasus.* This would have been a source of
constant irritation to the prince, particularly since the other
disgruntled officers in the ship were not reluctant to demonstrate their support of Schomberg.

Shortly after Nelson's wedding to Fanny in March 1787, at
which Prince William gave the bride away, Nelson dispatched
Pegasus to the Jamaica station, where a more senior officer,
Commodore Alan Gardiner, could legally convene a court-
martial. Nelson detached the sloop, HMS *Rattler,* to accompany *Pegasus* to Port Royal in a move to facilitate the court-
martial if Commodore Gardiner decided to proceed in that
direction. The presence of *Rattler* in Port Royal would assure
that there would be a sufficient number of commanding officers present in the Jamaica area to convene the trial, if that
was Commodore Gardiner's decision. Nelson also sent a letter to Commodore Gardiner providing the details of the dispute. The general thrust of his letter was not without some
bias. Initially he characterized the prince as a person who
"stands in a very different situation than any other Captain,"
and he further suggested that the incident that triggered

Schomberg's request for a court-martial was "trivial."[5] These were gratuitous comments that revealed some lack of objectivity on Nelson's part.

As it turned out, Commodore Gardiner chose not to fulfill Schomberg's request, and he eventually forced Schomberg to apologize to the man he detested. At that point the official issue of the court-martial appeared to have disappeared into the type of administrative "black hole" that swallows embarrassing situations, particularly those that would be discomforting for the Navy's senior leadership. Unfortunately, Gardiner's decision not to convene a court-martial did not by any means end the affair.

Schomberg was detached from *Pegasus* within a short time, and ultimately he was reassigned to a career-enhancing position as first lieutenant in Admiral Lord Hood's flagship, HMS *Barfleur*. It was known that Nelson had a high regard for Schomberg's professional abilities before he and the prince became embroiled in charges and countercharges. Based on Hood's appointment of Schomberg as his first lieutenant and his previous role as Schomberg's mentor, it is clear that Admiral Hood held a similar opinion. The difficulty at that point was with Prince William, who believed that both Nelson and Hood had failed to support him in his handling of the situation.

THE IMPACT OF THE AFFAIR

Nelson's handling of the dispute between Prince William Henry and his first lieutenant initially appeared to work to no one's particular disadvantage, including the Navy's senior levels. In the long run, however, it did not work out well for Nelson himself. When his former first lieutenant was appointed to *Barfleur*, Prince William was enraged. William even went so far as to write to Admiral Hood to complain about Hood's "support" of Schomberg; the letter triggered a testy exchange between the two. The prince was emotional: "I want words to express my feelings on this subject; was any brother officer of mine to require a Lieutenant to quit his ship, I should, my Lord, be the last person to take such a man on preferment. . . . your Lordship has given the Service very convincing proof of your approbation of Mr. Schomberg's conduct." Even allowing for his royal status, William's tone in addressing a peer and an admiral of considerable stature was intemperate. The conclusion of the letter reached dramatic heights with the inclusion of the First Lord of the Admiralty within the scope of the prince's indignation: "There is nothing in this world I feel so sensibly as an attack on my professional character. . . . Much as I love and honour the Navy, yet, my Lord, I shall beyond doubt resign if I have not a satisfactory explanation from both your noble lordships."[6]

Hood replied with restrained firmness, but the prince persisted, chiding the admiral for not consulting him before appointing Schomberg to his position in *Barfleur*. In this second letter, however, the prince called a truce, saying that Schomberg was "too contemptible for me to break off my connection with your Lordship." Hood accepted the truce, but not without a sharp observation: "How was it possible, Sir, as you are pleased to suggest, that I could consult your Royal Highness in the business?" Howe's rhetorical question could be interpreted two ways. First, he might have been alluding to the impracticability of communicating his intended action concerning William's former first lieutenant, since Hood and the prince were at the time separated by the Atlantic Ocean. Or he simply might have been saying that senior admirals normally do not communicate their intentions to junior captains, even those who are members of the royal family. In any event, the admiral, at this point, seemed to have fired the last shot, even if it wasn't a double-shotted broadside.

Nelson also added to the correspondence among the main participants in the affair with an interesting letter to Prince William written from Portsmouth in July 1787. Perhaps it was an attempt to balance his having placed Schomberg under arrest. Perhaps it was a matter of trying to smooth things over with a member of royalty whose support he was anxious to retain. And perhaps it was a sincere effort to mentor the prince, who was insecure in his command, primarily because of his lack of maturity. At one point in his letter, Nelson argued on behalf of the prince's former first lieutenant: "Schomberg was too hasty certainly in writing his letter; but, now you are parted. Pardon me, my Prince, when I presume to recommend, that Schomberg may stand in your Royal Favour, as if he had never sailed with you." After his recommendation Nelson gave weight to his suggestion: "Princes seldom, very seldom, find a disinterested person to communicate their thoughts to. . . . In full confidence of your belief in my sincerity, I take the liberty of saying, that having seen a few more years than yourself, I may in some respects know more of mankind."[7] Many a brash young officer has heard a similar comment from his senior, generally in less gentle terms.

THE BOTTOM LINE

After moving beyond the verbal jousting, we are left to consider the possibility that quiet, unofficial communications among those involved, but notably excluding Prince William, are what saved Schomberg's career. But it also seems clear, based on letters that until recently have not been cited widely in connection with the Schomberg matter, that Nelson's handling of the affair was the principal cause of his being placed on half-pay without a ship for five years after his tour in *Boreas.*

One of those documents is a letter from Nelson to his brother-in-law Thomas Bolton, written in November 1790: "If my brother and Mrs Nelson [the William Nelsons] are with You, you will know of my return from being as ill treated as any person could be for taking the part of the Kings son."[8] Admiral Hood wrote another and probably more telling letter connected to the affair to Nelson in November 1789. After saying that he had heard Nelson praised at the Admiralty for his active enforcement of the Navigation Acts, Hood went on to point out that he also had heard criticism for Nelson's handling of the Schomberg matter. He wrote: "[B]ut I am equally sorry to say that I have as often heard you censured . . . for putting Lieut. Schomberg under arrest—you well know my sentiments upon that subject as I candidly expressed them to you in several conversations we had together upon your return to England."[9] There is little doubt that Hood did not approve of Nelson's placing Schomberg under arrest.

It appears in retrospect that Nelson's attempts to satisfy all sides in a delicate situation failed all around. His friend and mentor, Admiral Lord Hood, who had actually presented Nelson at court after Nelson had come to his attention as the captain of HMS *Albemarle,* disapproved of his actions. There also was the strong feeling at the Admiralty, alluded to by Admiral Hood, that Nelson had acted improperly in the matter. And Prince William was offended because of Nelson's failure to support him more vigorously in the dispute. Finally, the naval leadership at the Admiralty could well have blamed Nelson for causing the situation to deteriorate to the point that it did. Nelson could find no vindication for what he no doubt thought was balanced and wise handling of the affair. It was another hard lesson to contemplate during his five years on half-pay.

THE EYE OF THE BEHOLDER

The Schomberg affair illuminates yet another element of Nelson's character: his tendency, at times, to see only the good side of an individual's personality. In this case it was Prince William whom Nelson viewed with, in some ways, an uncritical eye. During the entire Schomberg matter, Nelson not only treated the prince with deference, he also described him in glowing terms in his letters. Whether he was writing to Fanny or to his family, he described the prince in extremely favorable language and made only brief references to his negative qualities. In December 1786, for example, he wrote to Captain Locker that William was attentive to orders, and he expressed the wish that all Navy captains should be equally so. Despite many unsavory aspects of the prince's behavior, Nelson, in his own mind, held the image of a person with an admirable character and predominant goodwill, an image that did not match the reality. In the end, William was neither a paragon of admirable qualities nor a total rounder. He was dedicated to becoming a good professional naval officer, and he made considerable progress in that direction during his life. To Nelson's credit, he recognized that ambition on the part of William when many others did not. The difficulty in Nelson's approach to William was that he chose to ignore the less positive aspects of his character.

This tendency to construct a person with qualities considerably at variance with the behavioral evidence was one that Nelson also applied to some degree with Fanny, and one that definitely played a role later in his affair with Lady

Hamilton. Fanny was attractive and loving, but she clearly was not the paragon of idealized love that Nelson described her to be during their courtship. And even more clearly, Lady Hamilton's character fell short of Nelson's frequently excessive descriptions of her virtues, made to any and all who would listen. Whether this tendency on Nelson's part was an aberration in his basically strong character, or whether it actually was a quality that supported him in his extremely challenging career, is one of the more puzzling questions involved in the study of his life.

The West Indies. Although Nelson's activities generally were focused in the northern half of the West Indies, ships under his command operated as far south as Grenada.

This painting by John Francis Rigaud was completed in 1781, two years before Nelson began his tour of duty in HMS *Boreas*. It is the earliest authenticated portrait of Nelson and depicts him as a young man.

English Harbour, Antigua, painted by Nicholas Pocock and as portrayed in the *Naval Chronicle* in 1800. English Harbour was a base of operations for Nelson in the West Indies. Here he met Mrs. Mary Moutray, who became a friend, and her husband, Captain John Moutray, who was one of Nelson's antagonists.

Prince William Henry, from a portrait by Benjamin West as engraved by Bartolozzi, showing the royal sailor shortly before he was assigned to the West Indies as the very young captain of HMS *Pegasus*. Nelson's relationship to the prince was a mixed blessing.

The picturesque Caribbean island of Nevis, where Nelson met and married Frances Nisbet, as portrayed in Paton's *Down the Islands*.

St. John's Church on Nevis, known as the Fig Tree Church, as portrayed in Paton's *Down the Islands*. Nelson's marriage to Frances Nisbet is recorded here.

An unknown artist portrayed Frances Nisbet while she lived with her uncle, John Herbert, president of the council of the island of Nevis, and acted as hostess at his plantation home Montpelier.

©National Maritime Museum, Greenwich BHC2883

Frances Nelson was portrayed by the artist Daniel Orme shortly after her marriage to Nelson.

HMS *Boreas* under way in the West Indies. Nicholas Pocock, famous maritime painter of the Age of Sail, depicts Nelson's command during his assignment to the West Indies between 1784 and 1787.

Nine

Fraud AND Pardon

No good deed shall go unpunished.

—ANON.

wo very different situations toward the close of Nelson's tour in the West Indies added to his problems at the Admiralty. One involved an allegation of corruption in the process of supplying naval stores in the West Indies. The other involved the administration of naval justice in a life-and-death situation. In both cases Nelson attempted to do the right thing, and in both cases his actions resulted in unexpected and unpleasant consequences upon his return to England.

WILKINSON AND HIGGINS

In April 1787, only months before Nelson was to return to England, two merchants from St. John's, Antigua, by the names of Wilkinson and Higgins, approached him and Prince William Henry with claims of far-reaching fraud in the Navy's purchasing practices. Their accusations implicated both Navy and civilian officials. It is probable that the two men were aware of Nelson's strong aversion to that kind of peculation, and for that reason they selected him as their initial contact. Their accusations were aimed at merchants and civilian naval officials involved in the provisioning of the British naval squadron, as well as the naval dockyards, in the area.

The sum involved in the frauds was alleged to be in excess of two million British pounds. The prince was on the verge of departing for England, and since Nelson was acting naval commander-in-chief on the station—Admiral Hughes had returned to Britain, and his relief had not yet arrived in the West Indies—the matter was left with him for action. Somewhat reminiscent of the situation with the Dutch captain who had detained the British seamen at the Downs as Nelson was preparing *Boreas* for her departure to the West Indies, this was the kind of politically dangerous problem many captains would have skirted.

During his tour in the West Indies, however, Nelson had shown an ongoing interest in improving the Navy's contracting practices there. In several letters discovered when the naval dockyard at English Harbour, Antigua, was closed in 1899, he had questioned the way naval business was conducted on the station. In that specific instance he questioned approval of dockyard payments that were not properly supported by receipts. To improve the way the Navy conducted its business in the West Indies, Nelson had proposed certain changes to the Admiralty that would provide tighter control of the purchasing transactions by the senior naval officers involved.

Those proposals were not enthusiastically received at the Admiralty, where the comptroller of the Navy insisted that the old way of handling the purchases was satisfactory. In his biography of Nelson, A. T. Mahan, who himself had dealt with naval purchasing systems, suggested that resentment of what was perceived as meddling by Nelson was widespread at the Admiralty. Describing the official reaction to Nelson's suggested improvements, Mahan wrote: "The Comptroller of the Navy replied that the old forms were sufficient ... while all the civil functionaries resented his interference with their methods, and seem to have received the tacit support, if not the direct sympathy, of the Navy Board, as the Civil Department was then called."[1] The signal to Nelson from the naval bureaucracy was clear: If you continue to inject yourself into these matters, there will be negative consequences for you.

Nelson was undaunted by the discouraging response to those earlier efforts, and true to his growing propensity for quick action and his demonstrated dislike for administrative dishonesty, he took on the challenge with no apparent hesitation. He immediately undertook to assemble the facts of the situation. He began with a series of meetings with the two men, who expected to earn 15 percent of all monies recovered. The accusers apparently produced convincing documentation of frauds in the supply of a wide variety of stores to the Navy, and their evidence was sufficient to convince Nelson of the validity of their claims. Interestingly, the evidence also suggested that one of the two accusers himself might have been involved in the dishonest practices. However, based on the documentation and on his own judgment that Wilkinson was "very shrewd sensible" and Higgins was "a man of business" and that neither was "playing the fool," Nelson proceeded to inform the authorities in England. Of greater significance, Nelson was focused on the importance to the Navy of ending the fraud, rather than on the characters of the accusers.

In May 1787 he sent a barrage of letters to Prince William

Henry, the prime minister, the First Lord of the Commissioners of the Office for the Sick and Hurt, the comptroller of the Navy, the First Lord of the Admiralty, and the master-general of ordnance of the Navy. The letter to the comptroller was typical, and it summed up Nelson's motivation: "As a Fraud is likely to be discovered in the Naval Department under your direction, I think it proper to make you acquainted with it, that villany may be punished, and Frauds prevented in the future."[2]

Prince William supposedly proposed the scattergun reporting approach that Nelson used. However, anyone who has dealt with a large bureaucracy, particularly a military bureaucracy, knows that such an approach was likely to trigger a series of simultaneous, independent reactions within the naval administration. And those multiple reactions would not be appreciated when it was realized that numerous—and not always cooperative—administrative areas were reacting to the same charges. That circumstance in itself probably would have created sufficient resentment toward Nelson at the Admiralty to mark him as a potential troublemaker. Naval careers have foundered on lesser misjudgments.

As an indication that this was not to be a short-term unpopularity for Nelson at the Admiralty, it is relevant to note that many of the civilian officials and naval officers in that organization at the time of Nelson's tour in the West Indies would move on to positions of even greater authority within the British Navy over time. That was not a happy prospect for Nelson to face should the charges turn out to be baseless or, for that matter, if they implicated well-placed members of the naval administration.

In the event, Nelson's many letters informing of the alleged frauds, plus a visit to the secretary of the treasury, George Rose, upon Nelson's return to Britain, initially triggered official acknowledgments and not much more. A drawn-out investigative process that for years seemed to produce little in the way of results followed the acknowledgments. More than two years after Nelson forwarded the charges to the Admiralty, for example, a response from the master-general of ordnance had to be disturbing to Nelson: "With respect to yourself, I can only renew the assurances of my perfect conviction of the zeal for His Majesty's Service which has induced you to stir in this business."[3] Reading between the lines of that patronizing letter leaves little doubt that Nelson was being characterized by the writer, in less polite Navy vernacular, as "a loose cannon on a rolling deck."

Seven years after his return from the West Indies, however, Nelson himself indicated that some action had been taken on the Wilkinson-Higgins accusations and that he had eventually formed a positive attitude about the affair. He wrote of having "the opportunity of discouraging great frauds in the expenditure of Public Money, and as the Naval Storekeeper is punished by fine and imprisonment it is to be hoped a stop will by this means be put to further embezzlement."[4] This view of Nelson was supported by later reports by the secretary of the treasury. According to Rose, as a result of Nelson's initiative in the situation, the corrupt practices in the West Indies were corrected and all of Nelson's recommendations were put into effect. In addition, some of the participants were punished, although the most senior officials involved appear to have emerged unscathed. As with those in Britain who suffered financial discomfort because of his enforcement of the Navigation Acts, those who suffered for Nelson's exposure of fraud would have added their resentment to the prejudices against Nelson at the Admiralty and in other high places, forming a significant community among the naval leadership with ongoing animosity toward Nelson.

The initial indifference of the Admiralty to the allegations made by Wilkinson and Higgins became a part of Nelson's deep discouragement over his general relationship with his British Navy seniors after his return from the West Indies. His feelings are made very clear in a letter to his friend, Hercules Ross, written in May 1788. He writes that he envies Ross: "[Y]ou have got the start of me. You have given up all the toils and anxieties of business." And then he goes on: " . . . whilst I must still buffet the waves—in search of what? That thing called Honour, is now alas! thought of no more. My integrity cannot be mended . . . my fortune, God knows, has grown worse for the service; so much for serving my Country."[5] Finally, however, he says that he is still in hope of getting a ship. At that point in his relationship with the Admiralty, it could be said that he was sullen but not mutinous.

THE QUALITY OF MERCY

One of Nelson's responsibilities as acting commander-in-chief on the station after Admiral Hughes had returned to England was to convene courts-martial. In April 1787 he had that unhappy responsibility in the case of a seaman named William Clark. The previous summer Clark had deserted from HMS *Rattler,* the sloop commanded by Cuthbert Collingwood's brother Wilfred; it was a sorry affair. Clark had been sent ashore at English Harbour, Antigua, as part of a working party. While ashore he managed to get access to liquor, got drunk, and failed to return to his ship. During his subsequent unauthorized absence, he was observed in English Harbour, generally in a drunken state. Finally, on 5 July a marine from *Rattler* found Clark in the public market and arrested him. The marine testified at the court-martial that Clark had offered no resistance and "did not appear perfectly sober." It was a vignette that has been repeated many thousands of times in the navies of the world.

The offense of desertion was considered to be extremely serious in Nelson's Navy, even during the brief period of peace between 1783 and 1793. The mandatory sentence for desertion was death. The five officers of the court-martial included Nelson, Captain Holloway of HMS *Solebay,* Captain Newcombe of HMS *Maidstone,* Prince William Henry of HMS *Pegasus,* Captain Cuthbert Collingwood of HMS *Mediator,* and Captain Wilfred Collingwood of HMS *Rattler.* Their verdict was guilty, and Clark was sentenced "to be hanged by the neck until he is dead at the yard arm on board such one of His Majesty's ships as the Senior Officer shall think fit to direct."[6]

There are conflicting reports of exactly what happened next, but apparently at the request of Prince William, Nelson commuted Clark's sentence. At the moment before Clark was to be hanged, he was spared; then, in addition to sparing his life, Nelson acceded to the seaman's wish and discharged him from the Navy. Nelson's reasoning was a bit tortuous. He reasoned that once Clark was condemned he was, in effect, legally dead. When his sentence was lifted, he was by Nelson's reasoning a "new" man, and as such was entitled to be discharged, particularly since his former commanding officer assured Nelson that there were others in *Rattler* who could replace him in his former shipboard duties.

On a more personal level, Nelson wrote to the Admiralty that under the circumstances, he was convinced that if he had carried out Clark's sentence, "his feelings would nearly have been the same" as if he had committed a murder. In further defense of his actions, Nelson cited a previous case involving a seaman named William Ray from HMS *Unicorn.* In that case, according to Nelson, Admiral Hughes apparently had handled matters in a similar manner.

The sparing of the prisoner's life just before the sentence of hanging was to be carried out, notwithstanding the Admiralty's eventual disapproval, was an example of Nelson's approach to discipline as a means to an end rather than an end in itself. Many years later, in July 1799, Nelson would repeat the scenario when he spared a marine, John Jolly, just before he was to be executed for striking an officer. In this latter case it was believed by some that the sentence was commuted at the urging of Nelson's paramour Lady Hamilton, but upon examination, it is apparent that Nelson's sparing of Jolly's life was consistent with his behavior following the court-martial of seaman Clark.

Apart from the theatrical aspects of the situation with Clark, it was a vivid example of how Nelson saw even the harshest sentences primarily as a way of making a point. If the lesson was made to others, commuting a sentence on a rare occasion was simply a matter of humanity and common sense. In an era of harsh naval discipline, it is reasonable to assume that his handling of William Clark was an early and significant step in the building of Nelson's popularity among the lower decks of the British Navy, although clearly that was not an objective Nelson consciously had in mind at the time.

THE ADMIRALTY DISAPPROVES

In July 1787 Nelson duly reported the event to the Admiralty, pointing out that Admiral Hughes had left him in temporary command of the station when he departed for England. The reaction of the Admiralty was summed up by a scrawled comment written by the secretary of the Admiralty on the turned-down corner of Nelson's report: "Let him know that he had no authority to pardon Wm. Clark and that all he had it in his power to do, in consequence of the Prince's intercession, was to suspend the execution of the sentence till his Majesty's pleasure should be known."[7] It was another dart hurled at Nelson by his desk-bound, London-based Admiralty leaders for a decision he made on the basis of the local circumstances on a distant station.

Although the series of admonishments from the Admiralty certainly had a cumulative affect on Nelson, he continued to defend his actions in the seaman Clark case. A month after his initial report he was marshaling his arguments with the Admiralty. He pointed out that he had acted at the request not only of Prince William but also of Clark's commanding officer, Captain Wilfred Collingwood. He repeated that Admiral Hughes had acted in a similar manner in the case of the seaman who had deserted from HMS *Unicorn.* In the process of his own defense Nelson gave notice that he was not unwilling to argue over apparently obscure points of the law. But he also wrote that if he had been mistaken, he was sorry, and that "I only wish to know the exact rules of the Service in this respect." Apparently the Admiralty never took any further official action in the matter. It seems sure, however, that the Clark affair contributed to Nelson's sinking fortunes at the Admiralty. It was a classic example of the bureaucratic maxim: "No good deed shall go unpunished."

PART OF AN OMINOUS PICTURE

Whether Nelson's decisions concerning Wilkinson and Higgins and seaman Clark were militarily correct or not, there is little doubt that they played a role in his "beaching" by the Navy for the five years that followed his West Indies tour. There were no official reprimands, but there clearly was a growing attitude that Nelson was a troublemaker who had to be reined in, and what better way to do so than through conspicuous neglect.

Mahan in his Nelson biography summed up the situation well. He wrote that the Admiralty, "if slow to thank were quick to blame" and "if they could not recognize what he had done well, they were perfectly clear-sighted as to where he had gone wrong."[8] Many years later Nelson indicated that it was apparent to him that there was a significant level of prejudice against him at the Admiralty at that time. Again, Mahan sums it up: "Scanty thanks, liberal blame, and the prospect of an expensive lawsuit based upon his official action, constituted, for a poor man lately married, causes of disturbance which might well have upset his equanimity."[9] Fortunately for Britain, and many would say for Europe as well, Nelson's unshakable confidence in the correctness of his actions eventually combined with circumstances to bridge his long stretch ashore at half-pay.

PART THREE

The Woman

Ten

The Predecessors

Love does not consist of gazing at each other but in looking together in the same direction.

—ANTOINE DE SAINT-EXUPÉRY

*H*oratio Nelson was both a fighter and a lover. And the second aspect of that characterization deserves fuller illumination, not for potential salacious or scandalous amusement, but for what it tells us about the complex personality of an amazingly successful combat leader. Nelson biographer Tom Pocock captured the blend of the warfighter's side of Nelson's personality with his intense romanticism when he referred to him as "valiant yet vulnerable."[1] Over the years those two aspects of Nelson's character too often have been treated separately, for they were related parts of the complex naval hero, one who not only won crucial victories in battle but also carried on one of the most famous—some would say infamous—romances of modern history.

The eighteen months immediately before Nelson's arrival in the West Indies in *Boreas* are instructive when focusing on this aspect of Nelson's character. His romances in Canada and France, and the strong friendship with Mary Moutray that he quickly developed on his arrival in the West Indies, were milestones on a path leading to his courtship of and marriage to Frances Nisbet in 1787.[2]

In the months leading up to Nelson's arrival in the West Indies, two illuminating but very different situations arose during which he was headed directly for marriage; in both instances he reversed course. In addition, there was a close friendship with a married woman, a friendship presumed by most to have been platonic. This last relationship provided a model for the woman Nelson finally would marry. The three women involved in these relationships were quite different from one another, and we find no quickly identifiable pattern in their looks or personalities. Nelson's behavior in these relationships, particularly the first two, suggests that he may have been motivated more by a drive to be married than by the particular qualities of the women involved.

A common factor in all three situations was Nelson's inclination to hurl himself with unusual intensity into serious relationships with the women to whom he was attracted. Perhaps that inclination was related to his tendency to take a swift and aggressive approach to both the political disputes and the actual battles in which he was involved. In the years before and during Nelson's *Boreas* command, this romantic intensity became increasingly apparent. The intriguing question arises of how that part of his personality affected his brilliant leadership. Was it a plus or a minus in the overall development of his character? or in his combat leadership? Early clues to the answers to those questions can be found in Nelson's relationships with Mary Simpson, Elizabeth Andrews, and Mary Moutray.

MARY SIMPSON

In September 1782, just eighteen months before taking command of *Boreas,* Nelson anchored the ship he commanded, HMS *Albemarle,* in the St. Lawrence River just to the north of Quebec City. He and many in his crew, after five months of continuous convoy and patrol duty, were showing the classic symptoms of scurvy. The fresh provisions and the crisp early fall Canadian weather they enjoyed at anchor in the St. Lawrence were, however, quick restoratives. Although he was eager to return to England, Nelson soon began to enjoy the attractions of social life in the British colony at Quebec. He was graciously welcomed into the homes of many of the community leaders, where he made new friends. He was invited to social events, where he began to meet attractive young women. Interestingly, his reception in the Quebec community was very different from what he would find in a few months in the West Indies.

In that rejuvenated state of mind, Nelson met and promptly fell deeply in love with sixteen-year-old Mary Simpson, daughter of the provost marshal of Quebec's British army garrison. Mary was young, pretty, vivacious, and popular. Accounts of her exceptional charm and beauty were sufficient to deserve notice in the Quebec *Gazette,* where she was described as a "Diana" with a "noble and majestic air," and with "heavenly charm." Nelson's attraction to such a young woman can be understood.

Mary's popularity no doubt triggered Nelson's competitive side and added extra dimension to his strong physical and emotional attraction to her. But there is no evidence that Mary reciprocated the emotional intensity of Nelson's attraction to her. He was no doubt interesting company for her, and to be courted by a young Navy captain with a promising career represented a certain social achievement for a girl of her age. In addition, there was a potentially positive financial factor: A Navy captain could become rich in a single stroke with the capture of a lucrative prize. However, many other interesting young men also sought her company. As events turned out, it was a young army officer who eventually married Mary Simpson.

When operational requirements came to the fore again and he was ordered to sail in the company of troopships being sent to New York, Nelson was less than enthusiastic. For one thing, winter was not a pleasant time to be operating off the North American coast. At one point he complained of *Albemarle*'s sails being frozen to her yards. Worst of all, in a matter of only a few weeks Nelson had convinced himself that Mary was to be the woman in his life, and now he was to be parted from her. He was so certain of his love for her that when *Albemarle* was on the verge of heading to sea, he decided to leave his ship and his naval career for the purpose of "laying myself and my fortunes at her feet."[3] It was a surprisingly irrational and drastic decision on the part of a man with a powerful sense of duty, the ability to think clearly, and an exceptional naval career in the making. It is even more astonishing in the light of his numerous statements about the precedence of duty over personal matters that filled his future courtship letters to his wife-to-be.

In the light of much later events, however, it now can be seen as an early example of how a romantic attachment to a woman could potentially override Nelson's professionally analytical side. As with other important aspects of his character, this propensity to allow a romantic attachment to influence his professional judgment that emerged in Quebec in the fall of 1782 would reappear later in his career, when he met Emma Hamilton in Naples. For the immediate term, however, the outcome of Nelson's attachment to Mary Simpson also tells us something of Nelson's state of mind when he arrived in the West Indies a year and a half later.

Fortunately, a chance meeting on the waterfront intervened at a crucial juncture in the situation involving Miss Simpson. At the point of leaving his ship and throwing over his career to pursue her hand in marriage, Nelson happened to encounter Alexander Davison, a successful businessman and member of the local city council, whom Nelson had met during his social rounds in Quebec. His new friend was ten years older than Nelson, a bachelor, and, as it turned out, more levelheaded in romantic matters. Davison succeeded in talking Nelson out of a decision that would, in his own words, lead to Nelson's "utter ruin." Clearly he had a high regard for Nelson—later he would become his prize agent and confidant—and he probably sensed his potential for greatness. Nelson reluctantly listened to the forcefully delivered advice of his new friend, changed his mind about leaving the Navy on the chance that Mary Simpson would accept his proposal of marriage, and sailed in *Albemarle* for his new assignment in the Atlantic.

Nearly twenty years later, in a very different circumstance, it was Davison to whom Nelson turned to inform his wife that their relationship was at an end. On 15 October 1782, however, he was the man who talked common sense to a susceptible young man about to throw over a promising naval career for a woman who, as far as we know, did not reciprocate his feelings for her.

In the process, Davison's friendly but firm persuasion saved Nelson for his role as a naval officer who changed history through his strategically important victories. That accomplishment placed Davison among a small group of individuals who, at various times and under various circumstances, saved Nelson's history-making career when it was perilously close to a premature end. Later additions to the group included Nelson's stepson Josiah, who saved his grievously wounded stepfather's life at the Battle of Santa Cruz, and Earl St. Vincent, who saved Nelson's career after his humiliating defeat and near-fatal wound at Santa Cruz.

ELIZABETH ANDREWS

From Quebec Nelson sailed to New York, where he observed with disapproval that "money is the great object."[4] But for Nelson, a more positive part of the local scene was the squadron of twelve ships of the line, commanded by Admiral Lord Hood, that rode at anchor there. The squadron was recently returned from the West Indies, where it had participated in Admiral Lord Rodney's victory at the Battle of the Saintes. On the occasion of a visit to the squadron's flagship, HMS *Barfleur,* Nelson impressed two important people with his professional attitude, one quite junior in naval rank and one quite senior. The first was Prince William Henry, a midshipman aboard Hood's flagship, and the other was Hood himself.

Nelson had expressed his hope to serve in the West Indies, where he believed the opportunity for honor exceeded the opportunity for prizes. At one point he wrote of the possibility of gaining command of a ship of the line in Hood's squadron. Nelson got his wish to serve in the Caribbean briefly in 1783, but it turned out to be an undistinguished period, marked by a failed attack on Turks Island, before his return to England. The unsuccessful amphibious assault on Turks Island was an instance where Nelson's attempt to leverage a bold initiative into victory was defeated by a tough and well-led opposition. That scenario would be repeated at Santa Cruz de Tenerife in the Canary Islands in 1797, where he lost his right arm and came close to losing his life, and again at Boulogne, France, in May 1801. But it was at Turks Island in 1783 that he first had to learn how to get past a clear-cut military defeat of forces under his immediate command.

In June 1783 Nelson and *Albemarle* arrived back at Portsmouth, where the ship was paid off, and Nelson was placed on half-pay as a post captain without an active assignment. Rather than return to his home in Norfolk, he decided to travel to France, ostensibly to learn French. He took rooms at an "agreeable" lodging house in Saint-Omer, approximately twenty-five miles inland from Calais. There another set of circumstances triggered a new romantic episode. This time the object of his affections was Elizabeth Andrews, daughter of an English clergyman.

Once again Nelson decided that he had found his future wife. Elizabeth was pretty, had musical talent, and was seemingly more mature than Mary Simpson. Moreover, she provided consolation to Nelson on the premature death of his sister Anne. In November 1783 Nelson wrote to his brother William: "To-day I dine with an English clergyman, a Mr. Andrews, who has two very beautiful young ladies, daughters. I must take care of my heart, I assure you."[5] In December he again wrote to William about Elizabeth: "[H]ad I a million of money, I am sure I should at this moment make her an offer of them: my income at present is by far too small to think of marriage, and she has no fortune."[6]

It would not be the only time money would become a major factor in his love life.

In January 1784, however, Nelson took action to clear the financial barrier by writing to his uncle, William Suckling. He got to the point quickly: "The critical moment in my life is now arrived, that either I am to be happy or miserable:— it depends solely on you. . . . There is a lady I have seen, of a good family and connexions, but with a small fortune, £1,000 I understand. The whole of my income does not exceed £130 per annum. . . . will you, if I should marry, allow me yearly £100 until my income is increased to that sum, either by employment, or any other way?"[7] As a possible option Nelson suggested that his uncle use his contacts to help him find a nonseagoing position that would generate an income sufficient to facilitate the marriage. Once again we are presented with a surprising willingness by Nelson to compromise his naval career to accommodate a recently developed romance. The tone of the message was blunt and businesslike, but it ended on an emotional level that matched its opening, with Nelson wishing that "you and your family . . . may never know the pangs which at this instant tear my heart."

As evidence of Nelson's effectiveness as a writer and his uncle's generosity, Suckling complied with the request. The situation shows how, at the time, financial security was often dependent on family ties. But for reasons that are not apparent, the marriage never took place. Perhaps Elizabeth refused the proposal; perhaps Nelson had second thoughts about his feelings. It also is possible that he returned to England for the general election of 1784, which was perceived by Britons to be particularly important. There is evidence that Nelson might have considered standing for a seat in Parliament himself. In any event, we are left to speculate about the actual circumstances that ended the relationship and about what his career would have been like if the relationship had resulted in marriage to Elizabeth Andrews.

MARY MOUTRAY

Nelson's relationship with Scottish-born Mary Moutray represented an intense but very different kind of attachment. She was attractive, intelligent, and charming, but she also was married. In addition, at thirty-two years of age, she was more than five years older than Nelson. She was, according to some accounts, the mother of eleven-year-old twins, and she was the daughter of a British Navy captain. Of particular significance, she was the wife of John Moutray, retired Navy captain and commissioner of the Admiralty's dockyard in English Harbour, Antigua, when Nelson arrived there in July 1784 to take up his duties in the Caribbean.

The circumstantial evidence suggests that Nelson's relationship with Mary never advanced beyond friendship, although at least some of Nelson's writings suggest that he would, if given the opportunity, have welcomed a more intimate relationship. In spite of Mary's romantically unreachable status, however, Nelson's friendship with her probably was more important than his near-marriages with Mary Simpson and Elizabeth Andrews. With her combination of maturity, classic English good looks, geniality, and sophistication, Mary Moutray turned out to be the model for Nelson's ultimate choice of a wife, Frances Nisbet. And in the process she solved the problem he had complained of when he pointed out that there was "nobody I can make a confidant of" on his new station. This need for a friend in whom he could confide was not unimportant. History and studies of human nature have made it clear that even the most powerful and forceful leaders frequently need a trusted person with whom they safely can unburden themselves.

In an interesting twist, Nelson's close friend, Cuthbert Collingwood, shared the friendship of Mary Moutray. It was Collingwood who actually introduced Nelson to the Moutrays, and many observers believed that the bond between Mary and Collingwood was stronger than that between her and Nelson. Collingwood had preceded Nelson to the West Indies station as commanding officer of HMS *Mediator* and had transported the Moutrays from England to Antigua for Commissioner Moutray's assignment there. From his own writings it is clear that Collingwood was not enthusiastic about transporting the couple to the West Indies, in part because of the cost to him that was involved—a complaint similar to that of Nelson when he was required to carry Lady Hughes and her daughter to the West Indies. Despite Collingwood's negativism and his basically reserved personality, however, Mary Moutray was able to elicit his inherent goodness. They became good friends, and Mary's willingness to break through the exterior of Collingwood, a flinty Northumbrian, confirmed Nelson's opinion of her maturity and engaging personality.

A QUESTION OF AUTHORITY

Nelson's friendship with Mary Moutray could have foundered early, as her husband and Nelson quickly became embroiled in a conflict over naval authority. Captain Moutray, who was twenty-nine years older than his wife, had been court-martialed in 1780 and found guilty of the loss to a combined French-Spanish force of merchant ships that he was convoying. As a result he was relieved of his command and retired on half-pay, but presumably through influence, he secured a civilian appointment to the dockyard commissioner's position in Antigua. One of the unusual features of how he went about his commissioner's duties was that he continued to wear his naval uniform, although officially his assignment as dockyard commissioner was a civilian position.

This presumption became part of an unpleasant confrontation with Nelson, a man who took both his naval rank and the authority that it represented very seriously. In future years Nelson's fierce protection of his personal prerogatives as a naval officer would resurface. But with Captain Moutray it was an early test of his willingness to risk embarrassment or even censure in order to stand his ground against encroachment on his authority.

The problem arose not simply because Moutray chose to wear his naval uniform in his position of civilian authority, but because Admiral Hughes, as the senior naval commander on the West Indies Station, saw fit in December 1784 to designate Moutray as the senior *naval* commander in the port of English Harbour. That official designation precipitated the dispute, and the situation came to a head in early 1785, when Nelson arrived in English Harbour to find a broad pennant flying aboard HMS *Latona*. The broad pennant indicated that there was an officer senior to *Latona*'s commanding officer present, and Nelson, as the senior naval officer afloat in the area, had every reason to believe that was not the case.

Latona's captain was quickly summoned aboard *Boreas*. When Nelson learned that the pennant was flying in recognition of Moutray's claimed authority as the naval commander in the port, he sent the distinguishing pennant ashore. It was accompanied by a message saying that he would not place himself, as Moutray had ordered in a letter to Nelson in February 1785, under the command of an officer who was not in commission. Nelson wrote: "[U]ntil you are in Commission, I cannot obey any order I may receive from you."[8] In a conciliatory addition to his firm rejection of Moutray's naval authority, Nelson added that he would "ever be studious to show every respect and attention which your situation as a Commissioner of the Navy demands." And he did dine that evening with the commissioner at Windsor, his home at Antigua.

Nelson then ignored his own chain of command by going over the head of Admiral Hughes and writing directly to the Admiralty informing them of the situation and his actions. Subsequently Nelson was upheld by the Admiralty, but with an admonition that he should have referred the issue to the Admiralty through Admiral Hughes, rather than summarily rejecting Moutray's authority and Hughes's decision to grant that authority. It was another early example of Nelson risking his career by making an on-scene decision first and then anticipating confirmation of his action after the fact.

Interestingly, and in a somewhat comparable situation, ten years after the dispute in the West Indies with Captain Moutray and Admiral Hughes, Nelson wrote to the captains of several sloops under his command in the Mediterranean. The situation involved their efforts to suppress privateers, protect British trade, and support British garrisons ashore, and Nelson was anxious that his captains take advantage of the knowledge possessed by a uniquely qualified officer in the theater. The dispatch, which referred to the British naval commissioner in Malta, read in part: "Commissioner Otway being perfectly able to advise you on many points of service, which the present situation of affairs with Spain may render necessary, I am to desire that you will on all such occasions consult with the said Commissioner as well as receive his advice, respecting any temporary refit the Sloop under your command shall require . . . I have further to observe, that

Commissioner Otway's opinion of your conduct, will have a great weight with me, and I shall feel exceedingly obliged by his kind attention to my wishes."[9]

Nelson demonstrated a consistency of principle in the careful wording of the dispatch. He avoided placing a British naval captain under the orders of a commissioner, although by this time the Admiralty was appointing commissioned officers to administer naval dockyards and shore bases. He made it clear to his junior captains that they were to seek the advice of Otway, but there was no suggestion that Otway had any direct military authority over them. Nelson had avoided Admiral Hughes's mistake, while still managing to utilize the valuable knowledge of Commissioner Otway.

THE NATURE OF THE RELATIONSHIP

Despite their conflict, Commissioner Moutray was a cordial host to Nelson at Windsor, his comfortable home that overlooked English Harbour and its naval dockyard. And undoubtedly Mary Moutray had much to do with maintaining the relationship. In September 1784 Nelson wrote to Captain Locker about her in one of his first letters from the West Indies Station. The wording of this reference to his new friend stirs the imagination: "Was it not for Mrs. Moutray, who is *very, very* good to me, I should almost hang myself at this infernal hole."[10] Whether or not Nelson was inviting Locker to read between the lines, it is clear that he quickly had formed a strong attachment to Mary. Later, in February 1785, he resorted to superlatives in another reference to her: "Her equal I never saw in any country or in any situation."[11] Notwithstanding the suggestive nature of some of Nelson's letters about Mary, and very much to her credit, she appears to have been both loyal to and supportive of her husband.

Because of the closeness in their age—Mary could have been an older sister to Nelson and a younger sister to Collingwood—there was informality in the relationship that went beyond what one might expect between the wife of the dockyard commissioner and two of the commanding officers operating in the area. That Mary's friendship was shared with both Nelson and Collingwood was probably an additional justification for her willingness to pursue matters somewhat beyond the normal social expectations.

For Nelson, a desperate futility was attached to his relationship with Mary. She was somewhat older and, on the face of matters, considerably more mature, and her marriage appears to have been stable. Even her friendship with Collingwood stood in the way of something more for Nelson, at least on Mary's part, than friendship. Some people thought that she was closer to Collingwood, and that if she had become a widow in the West Indies, it would have been Collingwood whom she would have married.

SETTING THE STAGE FOR FANNY

In March 1785 Commissioner and Mary Moutray sailed for England. Nelson's female friend was gone after only eight months of friendship. The commissioner was in ill health and died shortly after his return to England. His death inevitably raises the question of what might have happened if he had died in Antigua, leaving Mary a widow while still in the West Indies. Would Mary have remarried to Collingwood? Or would Nelson have sought and gained Mary's hand, in spite of her closeness to Collingwood? In any event, after the commissioner and Mary sailed from Antigua, Nelson was disconsolate. He wrote to his brother William about revisiting Windsor after their departure: "I once went up the road to look at the spot where I spent more happy days than in any one spot in the world. E'en the trees drooped their heads, and the tamarind tree died:—all was melancholy. . . . By this time I hope she is safe in Old England. Heaven's choisest blessing go with her."[12]

Although it seems excessive for someone of Nelson's professional abilities and rank to be pining so effusively for a distant friend, his reaction was consistent with both his personality and his circumstances at the time. But most important, the departure of Mary Moutray, plus the two near-marriages with Mary Simpson and Elizabeth Andrews, set the stage for Nelson's meeting with his future wife. The combination of the basic susceptibility of his own personality, the circumstances of his two near-marriages, his close but constrained relationship with Mary Moutray, and the isolation of his daily existence made Nelson a strong candidate for marriage with the next eligible female he met. Such a marriage was a very strong probability. It was in that context that he met Frances Nisbet in the spring of 1785; in hindsight, the outcome of that meeting seems inevitable.

Eleven

A Young Widow

A good marriage is at least eighty percent good luck in finding the right person at the right time.

—NANETTE NEWMAN, BRITISH ACTRESS

Frances Nisbet was born on the West Indies island of Nevis in 1758, only a few months before Nelson's birth. Her parents died when she was only two years old, and her uncle, John Herbert, the president of the Nevis Council, raised her to adulthood. Herbert's home, Montpelier, was the finest of the seventy-odd plantation houses on Nevis and—a point of considerable significance—one of the few homes in the West Indies where Nelson was welcome. The stark white building, fronted with gracious pillars, decorated with gilt-work, and surrounded with tropical flowers, was set 700 feet above the small but busy harbor of Charlestown and the glittering, cobalt-blue Caribbean. It was an impressive and hospitable home in an exotic setting. The contrast between Nelson's taxing, day-in-day-out environment in *Boreas* and the gracious surroundings of Montpelier was striking.

In her biography of Nelson, Carola Oman included an evocative description of Montpelier's dramatic Caribbean background. "Nevis, viewed from the sea, resembled a highly coloured illustration of a treasure-island in a child's picture-book. It was almost circular, and its lower slopes displayed the sharp green of the sugar cane, fringed by groves of coconut. Its conical summit, of a much darker blue than the surrounding waters, was continually capped by the snow-white clouds which had reminded Columbus of the Mountains of Nieves, in Spain."[1]

A FASCINATING YOUNG WIDOW

It was in these lush and visually dramatic surroundings that Herbert's niece, known to most as Fanny, held forth as the hostess of the plantation and manager of the household for her widower uncle. And as events unfolded, not only did Montpelier become a refuge for Nelson, so did its young and attractive hostess. Fanny had been brought up on Nevis, and her father, William Woolward, had been a senior judge there. In June 1779, at twenty years of age, she had married the local doctor, Josiah Nisbet, who had attended her father during the illness that led to his death.

Doctor Nisbet became seriously ill shortly after his marriage to Fanny, apparently as the result of sunstroke, and the couple traveled to England, where it was hoped that the change of climate would contribute to his recovery. But unfortunately he died there in 1781. The couple had a son, also named Josiah, who would play an unplanned but significant role in his mother's marriage to Nelson, a much more important role than generally recognized. After their marriage and following the return of Nelson and Fanny to England, Josiah followed his stepfather-to-be into naval service and early in his career he saved his life at the Battle of Santa Cruz in 1797.[2] In 1781, shortly after her husband's death, Fanny returned to Nevis, where she quickly took on the role of the female head of the Montpelier household and became one of the most highly regarded women in the close-knit Nevis community. Her first biographer, E. M. Keate, referred to her as "a very fascinating young widow" who said little but did a great deal.[3]

Described as having "refined beauty," Fanny was very much a part of the British colonial culture in the West Indies, a culture that, unlike the American colonies to the north, retained its close political and social ties to the homeland. It is believed that Fanny, like so many of her fellow colonists, had been educated in England. Fanny not only was acclimated to the semitropical climate, she was fully integrated into the plantation social system of the islands. It was a relatively comfortable life, but one not without significant stress. The loss of her parents at a young age and the loss of her husband after only a few years of marriage must have been difficult for her. In addition, all the British colonies, and particularly the plantations in the West Indies, had gone through major economic difficulties during the American Revolution, when supplies as basic as foodstuffs were cut off. There is no reason to believe that her uncle and their home, Montpelier, were immune to these economic hardships. During one brief period before Nelson's arrival in the West Indies, Nevis had been under French control. That latter circumstance no doubt raised the general sense of insecurity of the British colonists on the island.

Along with her physical attractiveness and pleasing nature, Fanny Nisbet undoubtedly was a woman of strong character. In her biography of Fanny, Keate contradicts those who have described her as a timid person: "Nelson's own letters ... show very clearly that she was not a weak character caring only for admiration and excitement, but that she had outstanding qualities of intelligence and dignity, and, as appears very constantly throughout her life, the power of saying little but of doing a great deal. ... No doubt she won from others, as she most emphatically did from the great hero who was to be her husband, not only passionate affection, but also honour and respect." Keate, in putting Fanny in a more balanced perspective, also pointed out that her life on Nevis was not one of indulgence, referring to "the extraordinarily difficult and complicated conditions of her life when she returned to Nevis, presumably at the end of 1781."[4] This picture of Fanny is based on the evidence of her entire life. It appears on the whole to be a much more balanced portrayal than the superficial depictions by many commentators on Nelson's life, many of which unfairly tend to dismiss Fanny as an unexceptional interlude in an otherwise dramatic career.

Although she had developed significant strength of character and maturity during her young years and was very much at home with her son and uncle at Montpelier, Fanny lacked an important element of her life, something that potentially had great bearing on her future. She was missing the security and social affirmation that went with a stable marriage to a husband with at least adequate financial means and with a socially acceptable career. That lack was troublesome, not just in terms of her own long-term security but for young Josiah's future opportunities as well. Yet Fanny's chance of finding a good marital match within her social circle, no matter how advantageous her situation might have appeared on the surface, was not high.

Many of the eligible young men in the islands returned to Britain to find wives. Other young men among the islands slid into dissolute lives that made them less than attractive candidates for a stable marriage. Among the visiting naval officers the prospects were not much better. For one thing, the eligible young women in the West Indies considerably outnumbered the eligible naval officers who visited Nevis. Given the operating tempo of the British Navy's ships on the station, the free time in which serious affection and romance could develop was limited. In addition, heavy drinking and marginal behavior were not uncommon among the naval officers.

After near-marriages with Mary Simpson and Elizabeth Andrews, and a close friendship with Mary Moutray, Nelson was primed for finding love and marriage as he pursued his duty in *Boreas.* So too was Fanny, as she pursued her duties at Montpelier following her orphaned childhood and the premature death of her husband. Although it can be assumed that there was physical attraction between Montpelier's young hostess and the young captain of *Boreas,* other factors were particularly important to her in the long run. Among those, and perhaps even at the core of her attraction to Nelson, was the prospect of social and financial security for herself and her son. That emphasis on security would be a strong influence on her reaction to Nelson's physically risky exploits, and her lack of enthusiasm for his exploits was, no doubt, a problem for her husband.

In contrast, Nelson's love for Fanny was based—beyond mutual physical attraction—on his need for her emotional support, particularly for his career, which was at the center of his identity. This asymmetry of the most powerful psychological forces moving each of them toward marriage created, in the long term, emotional stresses that were fatal to the marriage. They had significantly different needs and expectations, but they shared a common difficulty in that the spouse was unwilling or unable to recognize those needs.

PRELUDE TO MEETING

When Nelson first climbed the road from Charlestown Harbor and visited Montpelier in January 1785, his focus was not on marital possibilities. The visit probably was a routine social event, and on the occasion the young captain of *Boreas* came away impressed with his host as "very rich and very proud," two factors that later would influence Nelson's efforts to secure Herbert's support for the marriage to his niece.

On that first call and the following one, Fanny was visiting friends on the adjoining island of St. Kitts. But during those initial visits, Nelson surely heard about her from Herbert, who was known to boast of his special regard for Fanny. He claimed to look upon her as a daughter, and one of the reasons for this closeness to Fanny was that Herbert's own daughter, Martha, intended to marry against his wishes and was not living at Montpelier. It is improbable, almost inconceivable, that he would not have boasted about Fanny to Nelson, to whom he immediately took a strong liking. It also is highly likely that Nelson's brother officers—those who had been on the West Indies station longer than he had, and who had met both Herbert and Fanny before he arrived—would have described the attractive young hostess of Montpelier to him. One can without difficulty imagine Nelson's curiosity about the young widow.

Fanny likewise had surely heard about Nelson before they met, but just as surely, it would not have been in a favorable context. Because of his various "scrapes"—

particularly the emotionally charged confrontations with local plantation owners and merchants over his enforcement of the Navigation Acts—he was well known among the colonial populace in the West Indies, generally unfavorably. And in a less politically charged context, she received a particularly intriguing report about the captain of *Boreas* in a letter from another of Herbert's nieces, who had sat next to Nelson at a dinner party at Montpelier. The report about "the Captain of the Boreas, of whom so much has been said," was at best a mixed review. Nelson's dinner companion described him in part as a person who was "very silent; yet seemed, according to the old adage, to think the more." It wasn't exactly the kind of verbal portrait that would pique the interest of an attractive young woman. Further on, the letter reflected puzzlement about *Boreas*'s captain: "It was impossible, during this visit, for any of us to make out his real character; there was such a reserve of sternness in his behaviour, with occasional sallies, though very transient, of a superior mind." Finally the letter reflected prescient insight: "Fanny, had you been there, we think you would have made something of him; for you have been in the habit of attending to these odd sort of people."[5] It would have taken an open-minded and perceptive woman to get beyond that rather negative assessment and attempt to "make something" of the officer in question. To her credit, Fanny did so, although it would be several months before her actual meeting with her future husband.

In March 1785, two months after Nelson first visited Herbert and missed meeting Fanny, *Boreas* reappeared in Charlestown Harbor. Once again Nelson called at Montpelier; this time he was escorting yet another of Herbert's nieces, Parry Herbert, whom he had transported to Nevis in *Boreas*. When the pair arrived at Montpelier, it was still early in the morning and the household was not yet up and about.

THE JOSIAH FACTOR

As if fate was intervening that morning, Nelson had an impromptu meeting with five-year-old Josiah Nisbet in Montpelier's dining room. The "silent," "reserved," and "stern" captain—the man who had created so much anger among the colonial population, frustration on the part of his military commander, and consternation with Fanny's female friend—immediately hit it off with the rambunctious boy. When Herbert finally arrived to welcome Nelson, he was stunned to find him playing under the dining room table with Josiah. Later Herbert described his reaction: "Good God! If I did not find that great little man of whom everybody is so afraid, playing in the next room, under the dining-table, with Mrs. Nisbet's child."[6]

Just as Herbert was mightily surprised at the scene of Nelson playing with Josiah in the dining room that morning, one can be sure that Fanny's reaction to reports of the event was quite different. What image could have been more endearing to a widow with a five-year-old son? It was a scene that instantly would have overridden a young mother's reservations about the reportedly "odd sort" of naval officer. And Fanny's positive reaction to Nelson's joining Josiah under the table for play would not have been based on a misjudgment of her son's implausible playmate.

Nelson's spontaneous reaction to Josiah was closely related to the genuine regard he increasingly demonstrated toward his officers, midshipmen, and seamen as his career continued to gain momentum. That wonderfully impromptu meeting between the five-year-old boy, who saw Nelson simply as a new playmate, and the publicly hard-edged naval captain was a brilliant, momentary illumination of one of the deepest and most positive strains of Nelson's character. In terms of the future, and on a less promising note, it also was evidence of his desire to have children of his own—unfortunately, a need that would not be met in his marriage to Fanny.

In turn, Fanny's appreciation of Nelson's enthusiastic and uninhibited attention to her son tells us much of her caring nature. Whether the couple realized it or not at the time, it is probable that the unplanned meeting between Nelson and Josiah actually sealed the union between Nelson and Josiah's mother. The first time they met, at a dinner at Montpelier, she thanked Nelson "for the great partiality he had shown to her little boy."[7] There can be little doubt that the thank-you would have been accompanied by a warm smile. In this situation Fanny and Nelson were reacting to the more sensitive sides of each other's personalities, in addition to the more obvious attractions of two young people.

AN INTRIGUING PERIOD

Between the couple's first meeting in March 1785 and what generally is recognized as the first letter from Nelson to Fanny that survives, written in August of that year, little is known of the intimate details of how their relationship evolved. However, there is intriguing evidence that matters did develop warmly, in spite of the exceptional stress under which Nelson was operating at the time and Fanny's inherent reserve. For one thing, we are told that soon after the initial meeting Nelson's close friend Collingwood informed Fanny "of the conquest she had made."[8]

Interestingly, we also know from Nelson's correspondence that between March and August 1785, he was still pining over the departure in the previous March of his friend Mary Moutray. On 3 May, for example, he complained at the beginning of a letter to his brother William: "This Country appears now intolerable, my dear friend being absent. It is barren indeed." But toward the end of the same letter he wrote: "I am just come from Nevis, where I have been visiting Miss Parry Herbert and a young Widow."[9] Fanny had not yet reached top billing, but the young widow of Montpelier was at least listed among the cast in Nelson's social agenda.

In the very last sentence of that letter to the Reverend Nelson there was yet another important line, one that tells us about the state of Nelson's affairs and his mental state between March and August 1785. He wrote of his confidence in overcoming those opposed to his enforcement of the Navigation Acts: "My trial comes on tomorrow, but I am sure of casting my gentlemen." (The term *casting* here is probably used in its meaning "to scatter hounds and cause them to circle in search of a lost scent.") A following letter to his brother in June confirms just how preoccupied he was with his conflicts over enforcement of the Navigation Acts: "[M]y time for this six weeks has been all Law." Under those circumstances it is not difficult to understand that, no matter how strong Nelson's new romantic attraction might have been, potentially disastrous legal matters had to be a significant challenge, one that Fanny and Nelson, however, managed to overcome.

One of the most intriguing aspects of the interlude between March and August is the couple's use of a secret code in their communications. If there was need for a code in their correspondence, it is reasonable to assume that the relationship had progressed beyond a purely social friendship to some degree of intimacy. The use of the code to exchange personal thoughts, which is mentioned by G. P. B. Naish in his collection of Nelson's letters to Fanny, is strong evidence that the romance between Fanny and Nelson began with a full measure of ardor.[10] It mostly is left to the imagination, however, to picture the private growth of that romance, among the luxuriant flower gardens and breeze-swept rooms of Montpelier, which carried the young couple toward marriage.

Twelve

Courtship

Easier than Air with Air, if Spirits embrace,
Total they mix, Union of Pure with Pure . . .
—JOHN MILTON, *PARADISE LOST*

Despite the lack of details about Fanny and Nelson's courtship, some important elements of the early stages of their relationship are discernible and provide clues to the personalities of both. For example, it is evident that their courtship was an intriguing combination of practicality and idealism—two contrasting qualities that were linked by genuine affection. Recognizing what went into those qualities of practicality, idealism, and affection adds to our understanding of both Fanny and Nelson.

Obviously, it was necessary for much of the courtship to be carried out in writing. Happily for those interested in understanding Nelson and Fanny as real people, rather than historical characters, many of Nelson's letters survive. And particularly because of Nelson's willingness to express his innermost feelings in his letters—something he himself recognized in his personality—what he wrote to Fanny in the months after they met is the best source for establishing a real understanding of what went on during their early courtship.

THE BEGINNING

The first surviving letter to Fanny was dated 19 August 1785 and written from English Harbour, Antigua. That relatively long letter tells us quite a lot about the person Nelson was at the time. Further, there is a great deal in that letter that suggests the person Nelson would become as a national hero. And in addition to the more obvious evidence in the letter, it also offers more subtle clues between the lines—indications that are just as important as predictors of the personality that would evolve.

My Dear Mrs. Nisbet,

To say how anxious I have been and am to receive a line from Mr. Herbert would be far beyond the descriptive powers of my pen. Most fervently do I hope his answer will be of such a tendency, as to convey real pleasure not only to myself, but also to you, for most sincerely do I love you and trust that my affection is not only founded upon the principles of reason but also upon the basis of mutual attachment, indeed my charming Fanny did [I] possess a million my greatest pride and pleasure would be to share it with you; and, as I am, to live in a cottage with you I should esteem superior to living in a palace with any other I have yet to meet with.

My age is enough to make me seriously reflect upon what I have offered and common sense tells me what a good choice I have made. The more I weigh you in my mind the more reason I find to admire both your head and heart. But come, don't say: "What a vain young man is this, 'tis a modest way of telling me I have given a proof of my sense by accepting him." No, to your heart do I own myself most indebted, yet I trust you approve of me for this obvious reason. "He esteems me, therefore he is the person I ought to expect most happiness from by return of affection, if there is nothing in his character or situation that renders it improper."

My temper you know as well as myself, for by longer acquaintance you will find I possess not the art of concealing it. My situation and family I have not endeavoured to conceal. Don't think me rude by thus entering into a correspondence with you, consider that separation from the objects we esteem lose some of its pangs by a mutual unreserved correspondence. Therefore if you think it right let me now and then be favoured with a few lines. The pleasure I shall receive with them, you will give me credit for.[1]

At this point, the letter launches into a series of newsy, frequently gossipy paragraphs. There was a comment about Admiral Hughes, who had been carrying on a love affair before his wife arrived from England, being "in high spirits at having left her Ladyship at Barbados. He is every day expressing his happiness. . . . Entre nous the A. makes quite a —— of himself in this business. I suppose him a bachelor instead of a married man with a family." There was a note about one of the other British naval captains in the West Indies whose attentions had been rejected by two women and who then took up with a third who "almost I may say hates him."

There also was a reference to news from home: "My dear father, brothers and sisters are all well." And included with the family news was a note that his brother William was the beneficiary of a £700 inheritance. Given Nelson's concerns about his own finances at the time, the news of William's inheritance must have raised at least a little envy on his part. In his letter he even mentioned the now-distant but still-remembered Mary Moutray: "I had a long letter from my good Mrs. Moutray who is well thank God."

From both the content and the tone of the letter we can be sure that Nelson was writing to a woman with whom he already had established a mutual understanding. The letter was an attempt to intellectually define the relationship that the young couple had begun to establish at a more emotional level. It was written with a sense of confidence in the new relationship, but also with a sense of seeking firm ground upon which to advance. And taken in the context of its time and circumstances, it was not, as some have suggested, an impersonal and detached expression lacking in deep feeling.

Although the syntax and vocabulary may seem stiff by modern standards, Nelson's words reflect a balance of propriety and genuine affection that was appropriate to the situation. Of particular interest, his words reflect none of the extreme egotism of which he is often accused; he seems to go out of his way to downplay his own positive qualities, and there is no boasting of his professional achievements.

At the point when the August letter was written, Nelson and Fanny clearly had already agreed that they wished to marry, and it is left to our imaginations to picture the events and conversations in the exotic surroundings of Montpelier that led the couple to their decision. Did Nelson seize the initiative at a crucial early moment and surprise Fanny with protestations of love, which he then followed up with an audacious marriage proposal? Or did Fanny gently lead

Nelson to a goal she had established in her mind at a very early point in their relationship? In all likelihood, based on the personalities involved, it was a happy combination of both tactics that led, at least for the time, to a mutual victory in marriage for the young couple.

PRACTICAL FACTORS

By the time he wrote his 19 August letter to Fanny, Nelson already had spoken to Herbert about his and Fanny's intentions to marry. For the action-prone naval officer who already had secured the love and commitment of his intended, going through the formalities with her guardian presumably was somewhat testing. This would have been particularly true in light of the severe pressures of his naval duties, which were compounded at that time with the contentious legal actions against him for his enforcement of the Navigation Acts. However, the social proprieties of Fanny's and Nelson's world could be more formidable than the written law, and Nelson knew that. He also had sized up Fanny's uncle from their first meeting as a strong-minded and influential person; Herbert's enthusiastic approval of the marriage and ongoing goodwill were essential.

But arguably the most pressing practical issue for Nelson at that point was financial. His father was a parson of modest financial means, and there was no estate or Nelson family fortune from which the couple could benefit. His income from the Navy was meager, and in times of military cutbacks he could, and indeed at some points actually did, find himself in an inactive Navy status on half-pay. Fanny's inheritance was modest, and at the time of her marriage to Nelson it had yet to clear all of the legal issues involved.

In addition, Nelson claimed, with considerable justification, always to seek honor in his professional actions rather than wealth from prize money. Unfortunately, his prospects for prize money, particularly during the peace between Britain and France that existed during his assignment in the West Indies, were as much a matter of luck as of his skill and daring as a naval officer. His bad luck during his tour of duty preceding the assignment in the West Indies was proof of how important a role chance played in the question of prize money. In one instance during that period, as has been noted, he had captured several ships off the coast of North America, which for unknown reasons never reached port with their prize crews. In another situation, the proceeds from a prize that he captured in the Caribbean actually went to the admiral of a fleet that had been close to the action rather than to Nelson and his men.

All factors considered, when Nelson referred to his "situation" in his August letter to Fanny, we may be sure that a significant portion of their necessarily intermittent face-to-face conversations included financial matters. And we may be equally sure that those financial issues raised worrisome questions for the young couple about the viability of their plans for a life together. There could be no attempt to marry and then somehow make ends meet, particularly because of the presence of Josiah in the situation.

Beyond Nelson's mention in his letter to Fanny, there is further evidence in his follow-up correspondence that he quickly raised the question of money with Herbert and asked whether or not they could count on him to strengthen his and Fanny's financial circumstances. But somewhat surprisingly, Herbert was noncommittal. Fanny could count on an inheritance after his death, Herbert said, but he could not do much immediately to help the couple financially. In the end, however, and after leaving the couple in suspense for a considerable period, he agreed to provide a modest annual supplement to augment their income.

RETURNING TO THE WELL

In addition to his appeal to Herbert, Nelson once again turned to his uncle, William Suckling, for financial help. In November 1785 he wrote to Suckling, at first complaining: "Not a scrap of a pen have I by the last Packet from any relation in England." Then somewhat self-consciously he began to get to the point: "[H]owever, you see I don't think I am forgot, more specially when I open a business which, perhaps, you will smile at . . . and say, 'this Horatio is for ever in love.'"[2] Then the appeal took on a tone similar to Nelson's earlier letter to Suckling about Elizabeth Andrews. This time, however, the letter was a bit longer, and the tone was somewhat less florid. There was an appeal to family pride by citing the presumed financial generosity of Fanny's uncle toward the couple, a not-so-subtle tactic to push his uncle to a quick and favorable decision.

Optimism and a sense of urgency marked the close of the appeal portion of the letter: "My future happiness, I give you my honour, is now in your power. . . . Don't disappoint me, or my heart will break; trust to my honour to do a good turn for some other person if it is in my power. I can say no more, but trust implicitly to your goodness and pray let me know of your generous action by the first Packet." Happily, the result was the same as in the earlier request concerning the potential marriage to Miss Andrews, and Suckling agreed to contribute to the support of his nephew and his intended wife. Once again Nelson's letter-writing skill and his uncle's generosity carried the day.

Although Suckling's response was affirmative, there is evidence that he felt pressured in the process. He wrote to his nephew: "Your application has in a great degree deprived me of my free agency."[3] In response to his uncle's chiding, to further support his case, and presumably also to clear his conscience, there was an assurance by Nelson that he was "guided by the strictest rules of honour and integrity." There also was an explanation for the lack of money that precipitated the request: "[H]ad I not been more ambitious of fame than money, I should not most probably [have] been under the necessity of making the present application to you." The matter of Nelson's preference of honor over prize money was a subject that regularly would recur throughout his later career.

As it turned out, based on the responses from Nelson's uncle and Fanny's uncle, the couple would not begin their marriage in desperate financial straits. The combination of income sources that had been arranged eliminated the economic impediments to the marriage, despite legal entanglements connected with monies that had been promised to Fanny and Josiah, and ongoing threats of lawsuits for damages against Nelson for his enforcement of the Navigation Acts. However, the concern about financial security that Nelson touched upon in his 19 August letter to Fanny came up continually in his correspondence with her, and became a recurring theme throughout the rest of his life.

In hindsight, if we read between the lines of her letters, particularly after Nelson returned to an active command in 1793, it appears that as the marriage developed, Fanny was disappointed at the modest financial returns for her husband's many combat exploits and the accompanying public acclaim. Nelson's failure to accrue even a modest fortune could well have been one more negative factor in a relationship that would at a later point come under other, more severe pressures.

THE HEART OF THE MATTER

There is no doubt that Nelson sincerely loved Fanny, and he had

the good sense to put that in writing early in his 19 August letter, when he wrote with simple eloquence: "[F]or most sincerely
do I love you." He then went on to define the quality of his love,
which he said was "founded on the principles of reason" and
also on the basis of "mutual attachment." It was an idealistic
presentation that smacked of seventeenth-century poets, particularly John Milton, in his descriptions of the Garden of Eden
in *Paradise Lost.*[4] And because so much of the early romance
was conducted by mail, the tendency of Nelson to define his
love in these idealistic terms arguably would have been intensified as he translated his feelings to the written word.

As he proceeded through his idealized rationale, Nelson
unfortunately provided ammunition for cynics by sounding
just a bit like a person struggling to convince himself, rather
than the object of his affection, of the depth of his feelings.
But given the plain-spoken clarity of his early declaration of
love, and given that Nelson was a person whose emotions
were almost always close to the surface of his personality,
there could be little doubt of the significant depth of his feelings for Fanny. The only question left after reading the letter
is how durable those feelings would be in the long term.

To that question about lasting love, the letter offers an
intriguing clue in Nelson's statement that, for him, living in a
cottage with Fanny would be "superior to living in a palace
with any other I have yet to meet with." There are at least two
potential interpretations of that statement. The first, and most
obvious, is to see it as a straightforward claim that Fanny was
superior, in Nelson's mind, to the succession of women who
had previously captured his heart. The second, and more
provocative, is the possibility that subconsciously Nelson
sensed that there would be a more consuming love in the
future, one that would surpass his feelings for Fanny, just as his
current feelings for her overshadowed those for her predeces-
sors. Nonetheless, there can be little doubt that Nelson had

formed a sincere and deep attachment to Fanny, and she for him, in the summer of 1785.

SEEING INNER BEAUTY

Nelson told Fanny in the August letter, "The more I weigh you in my mind the more reason I find to admire both your head and your heart." He thus bypassed more expected references to his love's physical charms to focus on her intellectual quality and inner beauty, showing his willingness to look beyond the superficial. His statement also suggests that he believed Fanny was capable of understanding his love at an intellectual level, and therefore he moved beyond the kind of compliment that might have been expected from a self-confident and strong-willed naval officer of his day.

Significantly, however, the reference also provided an important warning sign. It suggested that neither mere physical attraction nor a mediocre accommodation lacking in feeling would be sufficient to sustain his marriage. In addition, Nelson's words suggest that he would need very strong ongoing psychological support as much as he needed other, more emotional aspects of marriage. The line suggests his need not only to connect at an intellectual level with Fanny, but to draw upon her enthusiastic and unwavering support of his career. In the heat of young love it was a signal that was easily overlooked. In the light of events to come, however, it emerges as an indicator of a critical need that sadly would not be met by Fanny.

Thirteen

Marriage

Courtship to marriage, as a very witty
prologue to a very dull Play.

—WILLIAM CONGREVE

Although the initial paragraphs of Nelson's first known letter to Fanny struck a serious tone, one that reflected acute idealism, the chatty paragraphs that followed were much lighter. One of the more amusing of those paragraphs described the positively scandalous event involving "Miss Whitehead's desertion from her father's house in St. John's [presumably the town of St. John's on Antigua and not the island of St. John] to St. Christophers." This item related how Miss Whitehall had escaped through a boathouse window into the arms of Captain S., "a gentleman well versed in the business of carrying off young women."[1]

In later letters Nelson sustained that less ponderous tone. It was a quality that gave a bit of balance and at times a hint of playfulness to his more serious, idealistic pronouncements about his love. And it is not unreasonable to assume that balance in his continuing correspondence paralleled the actual circumstances of the developing relationship with Fanny. In any event the correspondence between the two lovers continued to shed light on important aspects of Nelson's developing character.

SALT WATER AND SOCIAL NOTES

One example of that lighter tone appeared in a letter written from English Harbour, Antigua, in August 1786, in which Nelson asked his intended: "[H]ave you not often heard that salt water and absence wash away love?" Then mercifully he quickly answered his own question: "Now I am such a heretic as not to believe that faith: for behold every morning since my arrival, I have had six pails of salt water at day-light poured upon my head, and instead of finding what the seamen say to be true, I perceive the contrary effect: and if it goes on so contrary to the prescription, you must see me before my fixed time."[2] The letter's tone was hardly one of an indifferent lover, particularly with its reference to being with Fanny sooner than had been planned.

Then in December 1786 there was a particularly interesting social note, one that must have pleased Fanny. Referring to Prince William Henry, the future King William IV, Nelson wrote from Antigua: "We arrived here this morning at daylight. His Royal Highness dined with me, and of course the Governor. I can tell you a piece of news which is that he is fully determined and has made me promise him that he shall be at my wedding and says that he will give you to me. His

Royal Highness has not yet been in a private house to visit, and is determined never to do it, except in this instance."[3] The participation of the prince in her wedding ceremony, and the special effort involved on his part, would have been a significant social coup for Fanny. And the prince's involvement on the basis of his friendship with Nelson would also have strengthened his standing with Fanny's family, and especially with her uncle.

This was not an unimportant factor, since on the face of matters, particularly financial, a case could be made that Fanny was marrying somewhat down on the social scale. Even Nelson seemed to be aware of that possibility; in February 1787, just before the marriage, he expressed his concern that he might be taking her from her comfortable plantation surroundings to a life limited by his modest income. His comment was made in the context of a suggestion by Herbert that Fanny and Nelson might delay their marriage. Nelson wrote: "I asked him when he thought I ought to be married. His answer [was] that . . . I might be united to you when I thought it most convenient or let it alone till we get to England. I objected to the latter . . . but I daresay Mr. Herbert will do everything that is handsome upon the occasion. I hope he will for your sake for it would make me unhappy to think I had taken you from a state of affluence to a small pittance. I never wished for riches but to give them to you and my small share shall be yours to the extreme."[4]

As it turned out, Fanny would go from the comforts and constant social activity of Montpelier to a much more modest and physically testing life when she returned to England after the marriage. It had been anticipated that the couple would live in or near London and spend a considerable amount of time traveling in the area around that city. After some time in London and its surrounding area, however, they made a visit to Burnham Thorpe, the modest parsonage of Nelson's father. Because of the emotional reaction of Nelson's father at seeing his son once again, it was decided that they would continue to live there, at least for a time.

In a memorandum written for the early Nelson biographer, Reverend James Stanier Clarke, Fanny described the circumstances: "When we went to Burnham Thorpe we had no thought of residing with Mr. Nelson as it was only to make him a visit . . . Mr. Nelson's joy at seeing this best and most affectionate of sons was so great that he told us that we had given him new life . . . and that we had better not have come to him, than to have cheered and then to leave him . . . this good old man seemed to suffer much at the thought of our leaving him . . . which made us give up entirely our former plan. Then we agreed to live together."[5] The affection that subsequently grew between Fanny and Reverend Nelson was to last until his death in 1802. The two remained close even after Nelson had left Fanny and moved on to his romance with Emma Hamilton.

A GOOD HEART

In many ways Nelson's letters helped to demonstrate to his wife-to-be that he was both considerate and caring. For example, in September 1785, shortly after they had met, he responded with sympathy and empathy to news from Fanny that her aunt had died. His words of consolation had no taint of artificiality when he wrote that he wanted her to believe that he understood and shared her grief. "I partake in all the sorrows you experience." With a slight change in the choice of words, Nelson's sentiment would translate precisely to today's "I share your pain" response to another's suffering. He went on to encourage Fanny to allow the passage of time, her religious beliefs, and the use of her reason to soften the loss of her aunt. His consolation undoubtedly was heartfelt and contributes to a view of Nelson that contrasts sharply with the description of him as a man with "a reserve of sternness," the description penned by a friend of Fanny after meeting Nelson at a dinner at Montpelier.

There also were frequent references to Josiah in Nelson's letters. They reflected both affection and a fatherly concern for the boy's welfare. At one point he looks forward to teaching him to read, and at another point he refers to "my little Josiah." In yet another letter he promised that Josiah would always be considered as his own child. Both the tone and substance of those references put the later, adult relationship between Nelson and his stepson in a sad perspective.

That later relationship began with Nelson taking Josiah aboard his ship, HMS *Agamemnon,* as a midshipman after Nelson returned to active naval service in 1793. The bond between the two matured happily as Nelson guided what initially appeared to be a promising naval career for Josiah. Josiah's actions in saving his father's life at the Battle of Santa Cruz added a special element to their bond, and Nelson himself spoke of how he owed his life to Josiah for his quick action that day. Eventually, however, the relationship foundered when Josiah became an ongoing witness to his stepfather's love affair with Lady Hamilton. It is not difficult to understand the young man's embarrassment as that notorious affair began and then flourished in the Mediterranean theater, and on occasion he went so far as to show his anger with his stepfather in public. What is difficult to understand is Nelson's failure to recognize how his love affair would distress Josiah.

Toward the end of Nelson's life he was estranged from Josiah, who had by that time thrown over his naval career.

Nelson expressed what had to be his bitter disappointment at the disintegration of his relationship with his stepson on numerous occasions. Perhaps the most poignant of those statements came in 1800 when Nelson wrote to Admiral Duckworth, under whose command Josiah was serving as captain of HMS *Thalia:* "Perhaps you may be able to make something of Captain Nisbet; he has, by his conduct, almost broke my heart."[6] In many ways Josiah's bad behavior as a naval officer, which paralleled the deterioration of his mother's marriage, was a rebuke to his stepfather for his questionable treatment of Josiah's mother.

Nelson's sincere affection and concern for Josiah contrasted with his lack of understanding of how his public affair with Lady Hamilton would deeply embarrass and hurt him. But at least for the time during the courtship in the West Indies, Nelson's regard for young Josiah would have enhanced Fanny's affection for him and strengthened Nelson's commitment to her. It was not until later years that the extremely positive influence of Josiah on the relationship between Nelson and Fanny deteriorated and became one of the elements in the breakup of their marriage.

THE ONGOING QUESTION OF DUTY

Undeniably Nelson's sense of duty was a subject of prime concern to him during his service on the West Indies Station. As a result, it was a topic that continued to appear in correspondence during that period. There were two basic areas in which the issue was relevant. The first involved the enforcement of the Navigation Acts and the second concerned how Nelson's sense of duty related to his marriage. In both instances that sense of duty was being tested and shaped on a daily basis.

In May 1786, for example, Nelson wrote a short note to Fanny from Barbados, complaining: "Had I not seized any Americans, I should now have been with you." At the same time as he expressed his frustration at not being with Fanny, however, he also speculated that perhaps he should have avoided the seizures in order to be with her. But he quickly added that he was sure that Fanny's regard for him was too great for her to wish him to neglect his duty. Then, as if he felt the need to be absolutely sure that Fanny understood that he was doing the right thing by placing his duty first, he went on: "Duty is the great business of a Sea-officer. All private considerations must give way to it, however painful it is." Finally he ended the note: "But I trust that time will not have lessened me in the opinion of her, whom it shall be the business of my future life to make happy."[7] As it turned out, Nelson was not able to achieve the difficult balance between his duty to his country and his responsibility to his wife that he was attempting to define in his letter.

Seven months later, he revisited the subject in a letter from Antigua. The letter described his activities in the company of Prince William Henry, and it appears to have been an effort to explain why he had not had a chance to call at Nevis, and in a broader context, why the career of a naval officer is unpredictable. As he began to wind down the letter there was a note of frustration: "[W]hen I shall see you, is not possible for me to guess: so much for marrying a Sailor." Then he tacked on: "We are often separated, but I trust our affections are not by any means on that account diminished." Finally, there was a closing statement clearly establishing the preeminence of duty in his life: "Our Country has the first demand for our services; and private convenience, or happiness, must ever give way to the public good."[8]

This particular letter also points out one of the most instructive qualities of Nelson's own words: their frequent, uncanny relevance to today's world. Nelson's thoughts about private convenience, even happiness, giving way to duty could be expressed by a twenty-first-century sailor about to be separated from spouse and family during a deployment. They go to the essence of the question: Is one's duty to service and country more important than the duty to family? In the case of Nelson and Fanny, the long-range problem for their marriage was that for one the answer was an unequivocal yes, while for the other it was a muted but definite no.

If there seems to be an excessive focus by Nelson on defining his duty to Fanny, perhaps his attention to the subject was brought on by things that Fanny had said. But in any case, he was anticipating one of the key factors in the breakup of their marriage. For all her good sense and genuine affection for Nelson, Fanny never accepted the need for her to constantly and enthusiastically support his career. For Fanny, his career was a means to an end, not an end in itself. For Nelson, his career and accompanying successes were the essence of his being.

Either because he understood his own makeup so well, or because he was acting instinctively, Nelson was sending a message about his need for clear and consistent approbation from his wife. Unfortunately, it would become apparent later in the marriage that Fanny either didn't truly grasp the importance of the message, or she chose to ignore it. In all likelihood, given the warmth she demonstrated during the courtship and her loyalty to her husband even after they were separated, it was the former reason. Perhaps the best example of Fanny's perspective on Nelson's combat exploits appears in a letter from her to Nelson after his heroics at the Battle of Cape St. Vincent: "You have done desperate actions enough. Now may I, indeed I do beg, that you never board again. *Leave* it for *Captains.*"[9]

With justification, modern observers of the marriage raise the question of whether or not Nelson provided what was needed from his side of the relationship for the marriage to prosper. Lacking a significant body of written evidence from Fanny herself, we have little upon which to base a judgment. Referring to the social attitudes of the time, on one hand, and Nelson's sensitive nature, on the other, we still are left with inconclusive evidence on the question of how much responsibility for the marriage's breakup accrues to Nelson and how much can be attached to Fanny.

THE SIGNIFICANCE OF MAIL

It is hard for a person who has not gone to sea to fully understand the importance of mail; without a doubt, receiving mail from Fanny was an important matter for her intended. In his August 1785 letter Nelson asks Fanny to favor him with a few lines. In early September he excuses her for not writing because of the death of her aunt, but at the end of the same letter, he again asks her to write. In April 1786 he writes about the difficulty of not receiving any recent letters from her and how that prevents a dialogue between them: "I must write what I know and not answer to what you say." In March 1787 his reaction to not receiving mail is extreme: "Never was poor mortal more disappointed than myself yesterday at not receiving a letter."[10] And so it goes; his letters are periodically marked with comments about how he anticipated mail from his wife-to-be and how disappointed he was when there was no mail from her.

Although seemingly a trivial issue, the alternating disappointment at not receiving mail from Fanny—at times triggering a mild rebuke—and the pleasure Nelson expresses when he does receive letters from her, is revealing. Notwithstanding the irregular system of mail, Nelson interpreted Fanny's diligence in writing to him, or lack of it, as a measure of her love for him. That reaction may seem irrational unless one understands the importance of letters from a loved one to a person coping with the isolation of life in an eighteenth-century frigate. And in Nelson's case, the need he felt for written communication from Fanny was intensified by his emotional personality and the animosity of the local population that surrounded him. Each letter anticipated and unreceived was a tiny crack in the marriage's underpinning, an accumulation of which would no doubt significantly contribute to the weakening of the marriage's foundation.

A LACK OF GUILE

If there were some notable weaknesses in Nelson's personality, such as his near-compulsive need for praise, there was at least an equal balance with truly admirable qualities that clearly were emerging at this time. And Nelson's lack of guile was among those qualities evidenced during his courtship of Fanny. Beginning with the letter of August 1785, there is no indication of even the temptation to be anything but perfectly frank about both his financial situation and the demands of his profession. He appears to have recognized the importance of those issues to the durability of his relationship with Fanny.

Even in Nelson's view of himself there was no attempt to conceal his potential weaknesses, and repeatedly in his letters to Fanny he recognizes his faults. In February 1786, for example, he pointed out: "We are none of us perfect and myself probably much less so than you deserve." In a later letter, one written just before the marriage, he acknowledged his own shortcomings and unwittingly foretold his and Fanny's future: "You have given me a proof that your goodness increases by time. These I trust will ever be my sentiments; if they are not, I do verily believe that it will be my folly that occasions it."[11] In that moment Nelson's lack of guile led him to foretell his very public indiscretions with Lady Hamilton and the resulting breakup of his marriage.

MARRIED TO AN AMIABLE WOMAN

Nelson and Fanny were married in the garden at Montpelier on 11 March 1787. Prince William gave the bride away, and the event was by all accounts a major social success. For Fanny, however, planning a wedding—the date for which largely depended on the whim of Prince William—must have been nerve-wracking, and it was an initial example of how the major events of her life would be subordinated to Nelson's career. For Nelson's part, he was still dealing with the angry reactions of the area's plantation owners and merchants. By all accounts, however, the event was a splendid beginning for the marriage, and one of the interesting sidelights was Nelson's receipt of a silver watch from the crew of *Boreas*. For any Navy ship captain, a gift from such a source would outweigh even the presence of a prince.

Following the ceremony there was to be no extended honeymoon, and Nelson quickly began preparing *Boreas* for the return voyage to England. Toward the end of March he was in a less than joyous mood when he wrote to Captain Locker: "[N]o man has had more illness or trouble on a Station than I have experienced." But quickly he shifted his tone and included a statement that put his marriage to Fanny in a positive perspective: "[B]ut let me lay a balance on the other side— I am married to an amiable woman, that far makes amends for everything: indeed till I married her I never knew happiness."[12] Fanny had, at least in the immediate term, taken on the support role for Nelson's career that he desperately needed.

Contrasting with Nelson's optimistic attitude about his

marriage as it related to his Navy career was an observation made by a friend on the day after the wedding. The friend, Captain Thomas Pringle, was reported to have commented: "The Navy . . . yesterday lost one of its greatest ornaments by Nelson's marriage. It is a national loss that such an officer should marry; had it not been for that circumstance, I foresaw that Nelson would become the greatest man in the Service."[13] In the light of events to come that observation was startlingly close to the truth, as Nelson's shattered marriage and related romance with Lady Hamilton could well have cut his career short. Pringle perceptively saw the conflict between the marriage and Nelson's career; but fortunately he was wrong about Nelson's career being brought to a premature end.

Interestingly, Pringle was not alone in his negative reaction to Nelson's marriage. Prince William, who had so enthusiastically given the bride away, also had reservations. As if sensing the career threat that the failure of the marriage would precipitate, he observed: "Poor Nelson is over head and ears in love . . . He is now in for it. I wish him well and happy, and that he may not repent the step he has taken."[14] William was observant enough to recognize just how important his friend's marriage would be to his future happiness.

ONE WONDERS

As noted, a coherent collection of Fanny's letters, the basic evidence that would facilitate an analysis of their courtship and marriage from her perspective, is not available. Based on the many references in Nelson's correspondence, we know that Fanny definitely wrote to him, probably with some regularity, but unfortunately there is not a collected body of those letters extant today. It was Nelson himself who burned most of Fanny's letters to him. Exacerbating that problem, the first full biography of Fanny was not written until 1939.[15] Unfortunately, there remain surprisingly few works devoted to her life. There is no doubt that her letters and additional serious biographies about her would sharpen our focus on the relationship. But for the present it is important that we recognize that we are judging a relationship primarily on the basis of the written evidence left by only one of the parties involved.

Fourteen

Aftermath

Between the idea and the reality . . .
falls the shadow.

—T. S. ELIOT

*J*ust as Nelson's official actions during his West Indies assignment turned out to have negative implications for his career, so too his marriage to Fanny began to take on disappointing aspects after their return to England. What started with idealism, high hopes, and warm affection began a drift toward coolness and petty complaints. Fanny wrote complaining about Nelson risking his life (and parenthetically her security); Nelson expressed his irritation over items missing from his sea chest. It was a drift that would bring the marriage to an unhappy end in less than fifteen years. All that was needed was a final blow to the union, and that arrived in the form of Emma Hamilton. In all probability, however,

Lady Hamilton was not the cause of the marriage's failure but an effect.

A TROUBLESOME WELCOME

Nelson departed from the West Indies in May 1787 and arrived back in England on 4 July. To his apparent disappointment Fanny had not moved aboard *Boreas* after their marriage, and she and Josiah traveled to England in the relative comfort of the West Indiaman *Roehampton*. After their arrival they took up lodgings in London, while Nelson continued his command of *Boreas* under a cloud of uncertainty.

Nelson anticipated that the ship would be paid off and that he would move on to another seagoing command, perhaps even a ship of the line. But at that point there was a shift for the worse in British-French relations, and it began to appear that war with France would begin again. In a letter to his brother in July, Nelson recognized that neither nation really was prepared for renewed conflict: "Although we are in a bad state for it, yet thank God, the French are worse."[1] Only three months later, however, he seemed more sure that war was imminent: "As to news, the Papers are all Peace; but, in my opinion, nothing can prevent a War."[2]

Based on that possibility of a resumption of war with France, *Boreas* was not immediately paid off. Instead Nelson was ordered to take on three months' worth of provisions on the real possibility that she would immediately be redeployed. The change in orders did not sit well with a crew that anticipated being quickly released from their ship after their three-year deployment to the West Indies. As a result, Nelson was faced with the embarrassment of a substantial number of desertions from his ship; it was a new and disturbing experience for him to be reporting that significant numbers of men from his ship had deserted. And it was a far cry from the situation at the end of his previous command in HMS *Albermarle,* when almost the entire crew volunteered to serve with him in his next ship.

In September Nelson and *Boreas* were still at the Nore in the Thames estuary awaiting further orders. By then, however, *Boreas* was being used as a store and receiving ship for impressed seamen—not the kind of activity that would please an ambitious and experienced captain. In fact, it would have been both frustrating and humiliating for Nelson. To make matters worse, there was the unanticipated separation from Fanny. At one point Nelson complained that he was "as much separated from my wife as if I were in the East Indies." As Nelson and his increasingly impatient crew waited, both Britain and France, as Nelson had suggested in July, realized that they were woefully unprepared for a return to war. The threat of war receded, and *Boreas* finally was paid off on 30 November. Nelson was placed in an inactive Navy status on half-pay, and remained in that unhappy position for five years.

A HINGE OF HISTORY

What followed the paying-off of *Boreas* was one of those intriguing, but little recognized, series of events that trigger "what if" speculations. In early October 1787 Nelson, while still waiting for a decision to be made at the Admiralty about *Boreas,* wrote to Captain Locker: "I have asked Lord Howe for a Ship of the Line, but *Boreas* is victualled for three months, and ready for Sea, ordered to hold myself in momentary readiness.... My health, thank God was never better, and I am fit for any quarter of the Globe."[3] With renewed health, and notwithstanding his tribulations with the Admiralty, Nelson appeared to be positive about his future prospects with the Navy.

Within a month, however, his attitude had shifted 180 degrees. It was reported by "a most intimate friend" that at that point, he "was so dissatisfied with the ill usage he had received, that I am certain, that had he possessed the means of living independently on shore, he would never have gone to sea again."[4] His immediate naval senior, who was in charge of all the ships in the anchorage where *Boreas* was located, was told by Nelson: "I now rejoice at the *Boreas* being ordered to be paid off, which will release me forever from an ungrateful Service; as it is my firm and unalterable determination, never again to set foot on board a King's Ship. Immediately after my arrival in town I shall wait on the First Lord of the Admiralty, and resign my commission."[5]

Fortunately, Nelson's senior officer took some quiet steps to prevent the resignation to which Nelson said he was so firmly committed, and the superior spoke to the First Lord of the Admiralty, Lord Howe, about Nelson's intention to leave the Navy. Howe, who then was prepared for Nelson's resignation attempt, apparently talked through Nelson's deep disappointment with the Navy and convinced him that he still had a future with that "ungrateful Service."

To demonstrate his high opinion of Nelson, Howe offered to present him to the king, which he did within a short time. It is another example of intervention, in this case by two of Nelson's naval seniors, to save his career. This series of events, little noticed in so many of the accounts of his life, leaves us wondering what the course of history would have been if Admiral Lord Howe had treated Nelson differently, or simply been unavailable at that crucial juncture in Nelson's career. How would history have changed if Howe hadn't reclaimed the career of the disillusioned and disappointed Navy captain who eventually became the hero of the Battles of Cape St. Vincent, the Nile, Copenhagen, and Trafalgar? The event also demonstrated that despite Nelson's powerful commitment to his career as a naval officer, there indeed were times when he was perilously close to giving it up.

THE HEALTH FACTOR

Added to the indecision and delay in deciding *Boreas*'s and Nelson's futures after their return to England in July 1787 was Nelson's continuing poor health, in spite of the brief periods of its improvement to which he referred. Several doctors wrote to him on the subject before his departure for England. In July 1786 Doctor Sholto Archbald wrote: "The situation of English Harbour is so badly adapted to complaints like yours that a continuance there for any time may not improbably be attended with serious consequences."[6] In May of the following year Doctor James Young wrote to Nelson about his health: "I am exceedingly sorry to find you give but an indifferent account of your health but I hope the change of climate you are soon to experience will be a means of restoring it to you again."[7]

The change of climate during the return voyage to England, despite Dr. Young's hopes, did not appear to improve Nelson's general health. A few weeks after his arrival at Portsmouth, he wrote to his brother William: "I have been so very unwell, with a violent cold, that I have scarcely been able to hold my head up till yesterday."[8] On 12 August he expanded on his illnesses in a letter to Captain Locker: "The rain and cold at first gave me a sore throat and its accompaniments: the hot weather has given me a slow fever, not absolutely bad enough to keep my bed, yet enough to hinder me from doing anything."[9]

This "violent" and debilitating cold followed by a "slow fever" that Nelson complained of was unhappily reminiscent of the "ague and fever" that had dragged him down just before his departure in *Boreas* for the West Indies. And there was still another physical problem with which Nelson had to cope: his eyesight was degenerating. It was a condition that resulted in the gradual increase of a film over both eyes. The degeneration continued to pose problems throughout the balance of his career, and at the professionally trying time he was living through after his return from the West Indies, it was one more stress-producing factor. All these physical problems would continue to varying degrees over the years.

THE ROUTINE MARRIED LIFE

Against this troublesome background that existed upon Nelson's return to England, he and Fanny began a routine of visiting various family members and friends. Apparently there was some consideration of settling down in or near London, but that prospect was overruled by Fanny's reaction to London's environment. Nelson touched on the subject in a January 1788 letter to Captain Locker: "I fear we must at present give up all thoughts of living so near London, for Mrs. Nelson's lungs are so much affected by the smoke of London, that I cannot think of placing her in that situation, however desirable."[10]

Eventually they moved on to village life at Burnham Thorpe, and in time, Josiah was sent off to a boarding school near Hilborough, where he would be enrolled until the time came for him to enter the Navy. For Nelson, the return to Burnham Thorpe was a return to his roots, and if he did not have a ship, at least he was among his family and neighbors in familiar surroundings. In that familiar environment he kept busy around the parsonage and the area, with periodic visits to London to seek a new seagoing assignment at the Admiralty.

The transition was very different for Fanny. For her the saturated colors of bougainvillea and hibiscus set against dark mountainsides, warm breezes coming off the Caribbean, a constant round of social activities, and a house full of servants represented home. But it was the stark Norfolk countryside, the bustle and grime of London and smaller towns, and eventually the penetrating cold of the Norfolk winter at the parsonage of Burnham Thorpe that displaced the things Fanny for so long had associated with home.

As Nelson had suffered from the tropical climate, now Fanny suffered from the quick weather changes and stretches of damp cold of Norfolk. Soon she was chronically ill and spent days at a time recovering in bed. While Nelson managed to keep active hunting, fishing, and, in the worst weather, reading Dampier's *Voyages*, he was never reconciled to his naval retirement; and periodically he used money from his very tight budget to travel to London and the Admiralty to press for a ship. His underlying drive continued to be his commitment to his naval career, rather than the quiet domesticity of life with Fanny.

Of great significance, there were no children from the marriage. Given his affection for Josiah, the paternal attention he paid to his midshipmen, the idealistic terms in which he defined his relationship with Fanny, and his emotional personality, this has to have been a major disappointment for him. One of the clues to how deeply the lack of children troubled Nelson jumps out of a passage in his "Sketch of My Life." In reference to his marriage, he wrote: "In March, this year [referring to 1787] I married Frances Herbert Nisbet, widow of Dr. Nisbet, of the Island of Nevis: by whom I have no children."[11] It is difficult to not infer bitterness in the final phrase of that statement, and one imagines how that bitterness must have contributed to the erosion of his marriage.

Another indication of the importance of children to Nelson emerged much later in his career and after his marriage to Fanny had disintegrated. In January 1801 Horatia, the child of Nelson and his paramour, Lady Hamilton, was born. It is clear that Nelson deeply loved Horatia. There is constant mention of her in his correspondence, and she held a prominent position in his final thoughts before the Battle of Trafalgar and his death in 1805. In a codicil to his will, written shortly before his death at Trafalgar, Nelson reflected his strong feelings for her: "I also leave to the beneficence of my Country my adopted daughter, Horatia Nelson Thompson; and I desire she will use in future the name of Nelson only." Nelson also spoke of Horatia as he was dying in *Victory*'s cockpit during the Battle of Trafalgar, referring to her and her mother as legacies being left to his country. Resisting the temptation to seek the most important factor in the failure of Fanny and Nelson's marriage, we may say that the lack of children from his union with Fanny was a major factor in the unhappy ending of their marriage.

THE MONEY FACTOR

Although Fanny and Nelson were not poor, their income was limited, and that placed strictures on their way of life in England. Nelson's half-pay from the Navy, coupled with the stipends provided by their uncles, was enough for them to travel for periodic visits among friends and family in southern England and then to take up a modest country life at Burnham Thorpe. But finances mostly were a limiting rather than an enabling factor for the young couple.

One particularly troubling threat to their financial equanimity occurred in April 1789, when a legal writ that was a carryover from Nelson's enforcement of the Navigation Acts was served on Fanny at their home. The suit claimed £20,000 in damages by American traders who had been affected by Nelson's enforcement of the acts.

In describing the event, Fanny painted a picture of a thoroughly incensed Nelson, a man outraged at both the legal action against him and the aggressive manner in which two burly process servers had delivered the writ to his wife. His anger was aimed at his naval and political leadership for not providing promised legal protections, and according to Fanny, he threatened to emigrate to France and "talked about joining the Russian navy."[12] Nelson's vehement reaction to the process servers and the repetition of his threat to resign from the Navy surely were triggered by the steadily accumulating negative circumstances he faced upon his return from the West Indies.

Further evidence of Nelson's frustration over finances is found among his dealings with the Admiralty. His problems with the Admiralty concerning how he had carried out his duty in the West Indies, such as the way he handled the Schomberg affair, were accompanied by frustrations over money issues with the Admiralty. One such was his attempt to gain reimbursement for his official expenses during the last few months in the West Indies, when he was the senior officer and acting commander while awaiting Admiral Hughes's relief. There is no evidence that he succeeded in his attempt.

DISAPPOINTMENTS FROM HIGH PLACES

After their first Christmas together, spent with Fanny's uncle, who had returned to England and taken a place at Cavendish Square in London, Fanny proposed a solution that might ease the couple's financial strain. She suggested that with the support of Prince William Henry, Nelson could secure an appointment for her as a lady-in-waiting to Augusta, one of the royal princesses. This would have seemed to both Nelson and Fanny a reasonable request to make of the man who had given Fanny away at her marriage, and who had continued to demonstrate his respect and friendship for Nelson. Accordingly, in June 1788 Nelson wrote to the prince: "I believe a word from your Royal Highness would obtain a promise of a situation in her Royal Highness's Establishment not unbecoming the wife of a Captain in the Navy; but I have only ventured to say thus much, and leave the issue to your better judgment"[13] The end of the request sounds very much as if Nelson fully expected the prince to use his royal influence with his sister to make Fanny's appointment a reality.

The extended separations between Nelson and Fanny that such an appointment would cause were not a happy prospect for the couple, and their willingness to advance the possibility to William was a measure of the strong need for relief from their financial pressures. In any event, whether or not the prince followed up on Nelson's request, King George III and Queen Charlotte would not allow Princess Augusta to establish her own household, and the appointment never came to pass.

Then in October 1788 Nelson turned to a senior navy friend, Commodore William Cornwallis, for help in getting a ship. Cornwallis was anticipating convoying a group of merchantmen to the East Indies, and Nelson emphasized his willingness to serve under him in the convoy escort. Five days after the initial letter, Nelson wrote again, repeating the same appeal; unfortunately, the response from Cornwallis to the two letters was negative. His response contained what must have been a hurtful excuse: initially, because he knew that Nelson now was happily married, Cornwallis did not "dare" consider him for an assignment; and now he could no longer do so. The realization by Nelson that he had missed an opportunity to get back to sea because of his marriage to Fanny would have been a hard blow. Whether Cornwallis's response was deliberately hurtful or inadvertent, the result had to be an increase in Nelson's anxiety about ever getting another ship.

The most distressing response from a senior officer no doubt came from Admiral Lord Hood. In May 1789 Nelson once again went to the Admiralty to argue his case for a ship to the First Sea Lord, Lord Chatham. When he was unable to get an audience with Chatham, he called on Admiral Hood at his home. The meeting was brief. Hood said that he could not press the First Sea Lord for a ship for Nelson. A shocked Nelson asked why, and according to Nelson, Hood's reply was that "[t]he King was impressed with an unfavorable opinion of me." Nelson's shock and bitterness at his treatment showed through in a letter to Captain Locker, written in September after the visit to Hood: "Not being a man of fortune is a crime which I cannot get over, and therefore none of the Great care for me. . . . and now I see the propriety of not having built my hopes on such sandy foundations as the friendships of the Great."[14]

The accumulation of poor health, petty admonishments from the Admiralty, and his rejection by those in high places upon whom he relied for support obviously weighed heavily on Nelson. When he arrived back in England in *Boreas,* he still retained his enthusiasm for his career, and in August 1787 he wrote to Captain Locker: "I begin to think that I am fonder of the sea than ever."[15] But within less than two years, according to Fanny, he was talking of leaving the British Navy and joining the Russian Navy.

SURVIVING A DIFFICULT TEST

The period immediately after Nelson's return from the West Indies was a unique test for him. He truly believed that he had done his duty well, and that he had served his country under challenging circumstances, particularly in light of the difficulties he faced with his own naval leaders and the local colonial populace in the West Indies. He pointed out to his brother William at one point that he had "smoothed the way" for the naval officers who would follow him on the West Indies Station. To the extent that he had confirmed the authority of the Navy to act decisively against illegal trade, he was correct. It also was true, however, that he left behind a residue of resentment among the plantation owners and local merchants against the Navy for what they determined to be unreasonable interference with their right to economic survival. That resentment undoubtedly had its carryover in a variety of important areas of influence in London.

Perhaps the greatest test of all was surviving the quick descent of his marriage into an accommodation between himself and Fanny. The downturn in the relationship with his new wife, matched with the decline of his fortunes at the Admiralty, would have been deep disappointments difficult for Nelson to bear. Unpredictability, even unjustified adversity with the Admiralty and Whitehall were all expected parts of the challenges of pursuing a career in the British Navy. But just as surely Nelson expected his marriage to be different; in his view, Fanny would have been the principal antidote for those problems. Then, as he saw that expectation dissolving, he replaced it with resignation and finally with a relationship with Lady Hamilton. Although there was little correspondence about his marriage during his five-year stretch on half-pay, it is clear that by the time he went back to active duty with the Navy in 1793, the relationship had deteriorated beyond recovery.

During his five years on half-pay Nelson very easily could have turned his active mind to business or politics. And he had, after all, spoken of the possibility of becoming a mercenary in the Russian service. Fortunately for Britain, and many would say for all Europe, he persevered in his naval career until matters began to improve. Eventually, in January 1793, he was given command of HMS *Agamemnon*. Twelve years later, Nelson would become the greatest naval hero in his country's history. And in the two centuries since his death at Trafalgar he has become the most widely written-about naval officer of modern times. Nelson's mentor, Earl St. Vincent, captured his preeminence: "There is but one Nelson."[16]

In sum, Nelson's three years of duty in the West Indies and the five years that followed were particularly testing for him, perhaps the most difficult period of his career. He faced stress and disappointment that honed his leadership and determination to a durable edge, one that would cut a swath through the naval forces of Britain's enemies for a dozen years—years that marked a turning point for the Western world.

Conclusion

If men could learn from history,
what lessons it might teach us!

—SAMUEL TAYLOR COLERIDGE

The most important thing about the life and career of Admiral Lord Nelson is that they represent a legacy. He is much more than an interesting and dramatic figure from the past; his life closely relates to our present and future. And if we have the patience and skill to illuminate that life fully and understand the basic lessons it teaches us, we will be better equipped to cope with the considerable national challenges of our own times.

THE OTHER SIDE OF HEROISM

Time has a way of stripping its heroes and its villains of significant dimension. As a result we often are able to revisit only the best or the worst, and the most dramatic, elements of the personality involved. This perhaps makes for more commercially profitable storytelling, but it doesn't help us to better understand and learn from the larger-than-life characters of our past. And understanding the full dimensions of those characters is essential to learning from their lives.

In Nelson's case, his early biographers constructed a heroic myth, focusing on the most positive and most interesting—to the public—qualities of the man. That was what the British public and its leaders needed, and it is what their historians and early Nelson biographers delivered. Then periodic debunking phases followed, during which the emphasis was on breaking down the mythology that had been created—in effect attempting to show that Nelson really wasn't that worthy of our continuing attention. That process of stepping back from the posture of adoration also was needed to prevent freezing a maritime nation, and particularly its navy, in the past, no matter how glorious that past was.

Between those two extremes was the real man, the person Tom Pocock called "Superman with Everyman's weaknesses."[1] That real person was someone who was much more than a naval officer who stood on the quarterdeck of his ship exhibiting a degree of fearless leadership that has set him apart from other military leaders for two hundred years. He also was a man who faced days filled with the relentless details of a naval life, the small stuff of his professional career, such as inspecting the material condition of his ship and assuring that she was properly provisioned.

He was a man who at crucial times made quick decisions and then stood by them through a long series of consequences those decisions triggered. He was a person who repeatedly impressed others with the quickness and penetration of his mind, but who also could be blind to the faults of those whom he loved or liked—or needed. He had the strength of spirit to press on through degrees of adversity that would have overcome others, but he was deeply hurt when he failed to get mail from the woman he loved. He loved his navy and his country, but vigorously and regularly denigrated their London-based leaders. In effect, Nelson was a man with an astonishingly nuanced character, one who must be seen in the totality of a complex personality—strengths and weaknesses, the dramatic and the mundane—in order for us to see the real lessons. The alternative is a barren repetition of platitudes to fill airtime and blank pages.

Learning the timeless truths embedded in that total picture of the man is the real challenge of studying Nelson's life. And applying those truths can be of benefit for those dealing with current national issues and those who will have the military responsibility for meeting future eventualities. Some of those lessons are clearly evident.

PROTECTING THE RISK TAKERS

One of the most important of Nelson's personal qualities was his willingness, or more accurately his eagerness, to accept risks as part of his job as a naval officer. The most obvious aspect of this quality was his courage in combat. By the time Nelson reached the pinnacle of his career at the Battle of Trafalgar in 1805, he had established a reputation as one who was fearless in battle. And that reputation was built in a full spectrum of combat, including fighting hand-to-hand in small-boat or boarding actions, mounting shore batteries under fire, braving the cannon shot and musket fire on a bloody quarterdeck of a ship of the line, and more.

Among the final demonstrations of that courage was his refusal to remove his very conspicuous military decorations from his uniform before appearing on the quarterdeck of HMS *Victory* at Trafalgar. That refusal made him an obvious target for a French sharpshooter in one of the tops of a French ship during the battle, and it cost him his life. But the physical courage Nelson demonstrated to such an extreme degree bought him the fierce loyalty of those who accompanied him in battle.

The second element of Nelson's risk-taking was his repeated willingness to put his career on the line in the process of carrying out his duty. This intellectual courage was a companion to his physical bravery, and it was clearly demonstrated by a number of his actions during his 1784–87 tour in the West Indies. Then and there he put his career on the line by defying his immediate superior and by risking the disapproval of the Admiralty's most senior leaders in London. In this particular aspect of his risk-taking he again earned the respect of those with whom he served, particularly the officers he commanded. They, more than any others, understood the courage it took to risk one's career in the Navy. The result was the formation of the Band of Brothers, men who were leaders themselves and who repeatedly contributed to important victories for Britain, despite frequently being outgunned and outnumbered by their opponents.

The lessons of Nelson's risk-taking for today's times are twofold. First, there is the crucial need to foster those men and women in our modern military who are willing to take risks to carry out their missions, whether in combat or in nonlethal situations that call for decisive action. In an era when political correctness has become an essential condition for political action and military promotion, this represents a particularly difficult challenge. The second lesson is that Nelson did not take risks for the sake of being theatrical. His risks were calculated. He evaluated circumstances, weighed options, and thoroughly prepared for the moments of truth, whether in combat at sea off Cape Trafalgar or in combat in a West Indies court of law.

THE REALITIES OF NAVAL POWER

It is an unfortunate fact that the adequate means for carrying out sound naval policies and important missions are often lacking. Nelson's responsibility for enforcement of the Navigation Acts in the West Indies was a classic example. He had a large geographic area to patrol, and he had a local population who played an active role in circumventing those laws. Anyone who studies the geography of the area within Nelson's purview will recognize that double the number of ships at his disposal could not efficiently have done the job.

In the United States today, this tendency to stretch a naval force beyond the realistic capability dictated by its numbers and its human and material resources is the result of building the U.S. Navy and Marine Corps to budget, rather than to the potential threats they must face and the missions assigned in times of national danger. The most disturbing aspect of this tendency is that periodically the lesson must be relearned at an exorbitant price, that price being unnecessary casualties at times of national crisis. At some point the elected bodies that have the difficult task of properly allocating a nation's resources must better recognize both the moral and the economic inefficiencies this lack of understanding of naval power perpetuates.

THE LAST PROFESSIONALS

Nelson accurately claimed that he served his country not for prize money but for honor. And although at times he complained that he did not have opportunities for prize money, it is clear that he sought assignments that were important to his country but that did not carry with them the potential for lucrative prizes. When he was commander of HMS *Albemarle*, for example, it was suggested that serving off the coast of America was an excellent opportunity for prize money. Nelson responded that he would prefer to serve in a theater where the opportunity for honor was greater than that for prize money. Prince William Henry, when describing his first meeting with Nelson, noted: "As for prize money, it never entered his thoughts."[2]

A comparison with America's uniformed military personnel of today, although not perfectly analogous, is close enough to be instructive. Those men and women serve, and sometimes die, because they believe they are protecting their fellow citizens and the values that are the bedrock upon which their nation was founded. That quality of basing one's career on a purpose that is far beyond financial considerations is among those that traditionally defined a profession. It is a quality that today arguably establishes America's uniformed military force as the last true profession in the nation.

LEADERSHIP

Leadership is an elusive quality. It is often confused with management, and also with charisma. In contrast, Nelson allows us to see true leadership, which includes the ability to motivate others to follow on a difficult course and in a variety of circumstances. In a military context the definition of leadership also must include the ability to win in combat.

It is important today to recognize and foster this kind of leadership, for in today's world we don't have the luxury of training up winning military commanders after a conflict begins. In an era that guarantees "come as you are" conflicts on a previously unrealized scale, it is crucially important that military leaders who will win in combat be in position at all times in our armed forces. And there simply is not the necessary emphasis today on encouraging war-fighters who will win in combat. The current cultural emphasis is in other, more politically correct directions.

Although many military observers focus on Nelson's tactics, neither his tactics nor the British Navy's significant technological advances of the time were the most important factors in his successes. In fact, Nelson's tactics were much less radical than many claim. He functioned beyond tactics and technology with a doctrine that transcended those two other important elements of combat. He also overcame budget-driven defense policies that were not very different from those currently faced by the United States and many other Western nations. Finally, he overcame the layers of civilian leadership at the Admiralty and Whitehall that frequently lacked on-the-scene knowledge and combat experience such as Nelson's. It isn't at all surprising that he faced those challenges; they seem to be built into nonmilitaristic, representative forms of government. What is surprising is that notwithstanding the challenges, he was able to lead his forces to victory in situations of huge global importance to his country. In the process he changed the course of history from the decks of his ships.

American sea-power prophet A.T. Mahan referred to Nelson as "the one man who in himself summed up and embodied the greatness of the possibilities which Sea Power comprehends,—the man for whom genius and opportunity worked together, to make him the personification of the Navy of Great Britain." Mahan also recognized his importance in saying that Nelson's name represented "not merely a personality or a career, but a great force or a great era concrete in a single man, who is its standard bearer before all nations."[3]

In seeking to identify the qualities that made up Nelson's unique leadership, the personal elements that made him the "force" described by Mahan, both the instinct to seize the initiative and the willingness to lead by example appear among the foremost. Both of those qualities can be discerned at their early stages in the young captain of *Boreas*. Perhaps the realization, not just of the importance of those qualities but of the importance of their being recognized and preserved in the career of a young officer, is the most compelling reason for studying Nelson in the Caribbean during the years 1784–87.

Chronology

29 September 1758

Nelson is born at Burnham Thorpe Parsonage in Norfolk. In the small waters along that Norfolk coast, Nelson develops his special combination of blue-water and in-shore seamanship, which becomes an important factor in his naval career.

26 December 1767

Catherine, Nelson's mother, dies. Her death undoubtedly leaves deep and permanent marks on his character, such as his "susceptible heart." Catherine's strong anti-French feelings also influence Nelson.

27 November 1770

At age twelve Nelson entered as a midshipman aboard HMS *Raisonnable,* a ship commanded by his uncle, Maurice Suckling. When Nelson's father, Edmund, asks Suckling to take his son to sea as a midshipman, Suckling responds: "What has poor Horace [Nelson's preferred nickname as a small boy] done, who is so weak, that he, above all the rest, should be sent to rough it out at sea? But let him come and the first time we go into action a cannon ball may knock off his head and provide for him at once" (Clarke and M'Arthur, *Life of Admiral Lord Nelson,* 1:7).

1771
March
He reports aboard *Raisonnable*

August
Nelson ships aboard a merchantman to the West Indies. Experience in the merchant service—not unusual then for British naval officers between assignments—gives him a broadened perspective on life at sea and the skills it demands. His experience in the merchant marine also contributes to an appreciation for the abilities of ordinary seamen, an appreciation not shared by all British naval officers of the time.

JULY 1772
Nelson returns to England.

1773
June
His participation in an expedition in search of an Arctic route to the Pacific further broadens Nelson's knowledge of the sea—and seamen.

November
Appointed midshipman aboard HMS *Seahorse,* Nelson sails for the East Indies, adding knowledge of that area's waters to his experience in the West Indies and Arctic Ocean.

1775
19 February

Nelson experiences combat for the first time. This engagement off the coast of India, between *Seahorse* and a local ally of the French, acquaints Nelson with the battle efficiency of a well-trained British Navy crew and a hard-fought victory at sea.

December

Nelson falls ill from malaria, a disease that probably contributed to his many health problems over the course of his life.

1776
March

As a patient, Nelson sails for England aboard HMS *Dolphin.* During this voyage he comes close to dying. Following a period of deep depression about his career prospects, a spiritual experience convinces him that he will become a hero in the service of his king and country.

September

Nelson is appointed acting lieutenant aboard HMS *Worcester.*

9 APRIL 1777

Nelson receives permanent promotion to lieutenant and gets assigned to HMS *Lowestoffe* for duty in the West Indies. The ship's captain, William Locker, makes a strong impression on the young lieutenant and becomes a mentor and lifelong friend to him.

1778
September

Nelson is appointed first lieutenant in HMS *Bristol.*

December

Nelson assumes his first command, HMS *Badger.* This tour of duty gets only one paragraph in his "Sketch of My Life," and generally little discussion by his biographers, but anyone who has gone to sea knows that it had to be a defining experience for the future admiral.

11 JUNE 1779
Nelson becomes post captain at twenty years of age. He is appointed to command HMS *Hinchinbrooke.*

1780
January
Nelson leads the naval portion of an unsuccessful attack on Fort San Juan in Nicaragua, the first of many actions that involve joint efforts with the British Army. During the operation, Nelson demonstrates the exceptional personal drive that distinguishes him in future military operations.

April
Nelson is given command of HMS *Janus* and suffers through a major illness, presumably a recurrence of malaria, one of many physical challenges he overcomes during his career.

December
Nelson returns to Britain.

AUGUST 1781
Nelson assumes command of HMS *Albemarle* and conducts merchant ship convoy duty in the Baltic, again extending his geographic experience.

NOVEMBER 1782
Before his return to the West Indies, Nelson serves in Lord Hood's squadron operating off the northeast coast of North America, adding still another operational area to his experience.

1783
March
Nelson fails in an attack on Turks Island in the West Indies. This failure presages other failures later in his career, such as at Santa Cruz in the Canary Islands and Boulogne, France.

June

Nelson Returns to Britain.

October

Nelson commences a four-month visit to Saint-Omer, France.

1784

March

Nelson takes command of HMS *Boreas* and sails for the West Indies.

4 July

Nelson arrives in the West Indies. This formative assignment includes contentious disputes with his military commander in the area, the civilian colonial officials, and the local plantation owners and merchants. In some instances the disputes focus on Nelson's authority on the station and in other instances on his vigorous enforcement of Britain's Navigation Acts.

MAY 1785

Nelson meets his wife-to-be, Frances Nisbet, a young widow in Nevis, West Indies, where she lives with her son. Nelson's early letters to her dramatically demonstrate his emotional side. They also are extremely poignant in light of the unhappy ending of their relationship and his notorious romance with Emma Hamilton.

NOVEMBER 1786

Nelson begins a brief assignment as aide to Prince William Henry, Duke of Clarence (later King William IV, who came to be known as the "Sailor King"). This assignment plays a significant role in the latter portion of his duty in the West Indies, and his connection with Prince William Henry continues throughout Nelson's life.

1787

March

Nelson marries Frances Nisbet in Nevis.

July

Nelson returns with his wife, Fanny, to England, where Nelson remains for five years on half-pay and without a navy assignment. This difficult period could have ended Nelson's career.

1793
January
Nelson is appointed to command HMS *Agamemnon.*

February
War between Britain and France is renewed.

June
Nelson sails for the Mediterranean and blockade duty off Toulon.

September
Nelson meets Sir William and Lady Hamilton in Naples, where Sir William is ambassador to the Kingdom of the Two Sicilies.

JANUARY 1794
Corsican naval campaign begins. During the campaign, flying debris from a cannon shot results in the loss of sight in his right eye.

MARCH 1795
Nelson distinguishes himself in action off Genoa against the French ship *Ça Ira.*

1796
March
Nelson reaches rank of commodore. At this point Nelson begins his career as a superb leader of fleet units in combat.

May
Nelson is transferred to HMS *Captain.*

1797
14 February
Nelson's participation in the Battle of Cape St. Vincent leads to his

being created Knight of Bath followed by his promotion to rear admiral.

July

Nelson leads boat actions off Cadiz harbor involving hand-to-hand combat.

24 July

Nelson leads a disastrous amphibious assault on Santa Cruz de Tenerife. The Spanish army and militia forces, led by a tough and resourceful Castilian general, Antonio Gutiérrez, inflict heavy casualties on the British. During the attack, Nelson's right arm is wounded and quickly amputated. With his confidence badly shaken, Nelson returns to Britain, where Lady Nelson nurses him back to health.

1798

March

Nelson hoists his rear admiral's flag in HMS *Vanguard,* and joins the fleet commanded by Admiral Sir John Jervis—by then Earl St. Vincent—off Cadiz. He is selected over more senior admirals for an independent Mediterranean command charged with locating a French invasion fleet with Napoleon embarked.

1 August

Nelson locates the French battle fleet—after a nerve-wracking, crisscrossing search of the eastern Mediterranean—just east of Alexandria in Abukir Bay. Using the aggressive tactics for which he becomes famous, he destroys all but two of the thirteen French ships of the line. His refusal, after receiving a serious head wound, to take precedence over others being treated by the ship's surgeon adds to his reputation among his men. As an aftermath of the concussion, Nelson suffers continual physical problems.

22 September

Nelson receives a tremendous welcome in Naples. Following the Battle of the Nile, Nelson focuses on supporting the Kingdom of the

Two Sicilies against French military pressure. During this time his romance with Lady Hamilton begins, and many at the Admiralty and Whitehall develop serious concerns about the impact of that relationship on his professional judgment.

November
Nelson is created Baron Nelson of the Nile for his extraordinary victory at the Battle of the Nile.

December
Nelson rescues the royal family of the Kingdom of the Two Sicilies from French troops approaching Naples and moves the Neapolitan Court, plus Sir William and Lady Hamilton, to Palermo from Naples.

1799
June
Nelson returns to Naples as the French are abandoning that city. One of his first actions is to cancel a treaty between the Neapolitan Royalists and the remnants of the French army and local rebels. During this period Nelson receives criticism for his approval of the summary execution of Admiral Caracciolo and the dumping of his body into the harbor.

July
In order to remain in Palermo, Nelson disobeys orders from his commander-in-chief, Admiral Lord Keith, to sail to Minorca. At this time, Palermo is the temporary location of the court of the Kingdom of the Two Sicilies—and Lady Hamilton.

August
Nelson is named duke of Bronté by the king of the Kingdom of the Two Sicilies.

1800
February
Nelson captures *Le Généreux,* one of two French ships of the line that escaped after the Battle of the Nile.

July

Nelson begins his return home overland in the company of Sir William and Lady Hamilton, adding fuel to the scandal over his affair with Lady Hamilton.

1801

January

Nelson is promoted to vice admiral.

Lord and Lady Nelson separate.

Nelson hoists his flag in HMS *San Josef.*

February

Horatia, daughter of Nelson and Lady Hamilton, is born.

March

Nelson departs for the Baltic under the command of Admiral Sir Hyde Parker.

2 April

Nelson leads the attacking British squadron in the Battle of Copenhagen. At the battle's height he disregards Hyde Parker's signal to withdraw, pressing on until victory is in hand. Then, in tough truce negotiations, he achieves an important strategic victory for Britain.

May

Nelson is created Viscount Nelson of the Nile and Burnham Thorpe.

August

Nelson leads an unsuccessful attack on a portion of a French invasion force assembled at Boulogne.

1 October

France and Britain sign an armistice.

22 October

Nelson joins Sir William and Lady Hamilton at Merton, a home he purchased for himself and the Hamiltons.

27 MARCH 1802

Britain and France agree to the Treaty of Amiens.

1803

16 May

War between Britain and France is renewed.

18 May

Nelson hoists his flag in HMS *Victory* as commander-in-chief in the Mediterranean. In July he joins the British fleet off Toulon to help maintain a blockade intended to lure the French fleet into action.

August

The French prepare to invade Britain.

DECEMBER 1804

Spain declares war on Britain.

1805

April–July

Nelson chases the French fleet, which is led by Admiral Villeneuve, to the West Indies and back. A few months later Villeneuve becomes Nelson's opponent at the Battle of Trafalgar.

August–September

Nelson returns to Britain for his last leave at Merton.

14 September

Nelson rejoins HMS *Victory* and, two weeks later, takes command of the British fleet off Cadiz.

21 October

Nelson leads the British fleet against a combined French-Spanish fleet in the Battle of Trafalgar. This battle exemplifies Nelson's thorough briefing of his captains and his reliance on the fighting superiority of the British Navy's seamen in close combat at sea. During the battle a French sniper's bullet mortally wounds

Nelson. The victory energizes Britain at a crucial time in its struggle with Napoleon.

9 JANUARY 1806
Nelson is buried in London directly under the dome of St. Paul's Cathedral.

Notes

Chapter 1. Pivot Point of a Career

1. Sir Nicholas Harris Nicolas, ed., *The Dispatches and Letters of Lord Nelson,* vol. 1, reprint ed. (London: Chatham Publishing, 1997), 100.
2. Ibid., 11.
3. Tom Pocock, *The Young Nelson in the Americas* (London: Collins, 1980), 17.
4. The West Indies generally are considered to include the crescent-shaped string of Caribbean islands, extending from the Virgin Islands at the north end to Grenada at the south end. In the northern half of the crescent are the Leeward Islands, consisting of St. Thomas, St. John, Tortola, Virgin Gorda, St. Croix, Anguilla, St. Maarten/St. Martin, St. Barthélemy, Barbuda, St. Kitts, Nevis, Antigua, Guadeloupe, Dominica, and many smaller islands. In the southern half of the crescent are the Windward Islands, including Martinique, St. Lucia, St. Vincent, Barbados, Grenada, and many smaller islands.

Although most of Nelson's activities in *Boreas* appear to have been in the Leeward Islands, his correspondence indicates that at one time or another he operated throughout the Windward Islands as well.

5. Nicolas, ed., *Dispatches and Letters of Lord Nelson,* vol. 1, 103.

6. Ibid., 104.

7. Post captain was a rank in the British Navy for an officer entitled to command a post ship (a ship of twenty or more guns). Once an officer was entered on the list of post captains, his promotions were strictly in order of seniority and were based on the death or retirement of officers senior to him on the list.

8. See Pocock, *Young Nelson in the Americas,* 44–124, for a description of the attack on Fort San Juan in Nicaragua.

9. Nicolas, ed., *Dispatches and Letters of Lord Nelson,* vol. 1, 102.

10. Richard Woodman, *The Sea Warriors* (London: Constable, 2001), 5.

11. Captain A. T. Mahan, *The Life of Nelson* vol. 1 (London: Sampson Low, Marston, and Co., 1897), 52.

12. David Howarth and Stephen Howarth, *Nelson: The Immortal Memory* (London: J. M. Dent and Sons, 1988), 3.

13. Nicolas, ed., *Dispatches and Letters of Lord Nelson,* vol. 1, 187.

CHAPTER 2. WORLD WITHIN A WORLD

1. Nicolas, ed., *Dispatches and Letters of Lord Nelson,* vol. 3, 40.

2. Ibid., 98.

3. Robert Gardiner, *Frigates of the Napoleonic Wars* (London: Chatham Publishing, 2000), 152.

4. Nicolas, ed., *Dispatches and Letters of Lord Nelson,* vol. 1, 112.

5. Ibid., 142.

6. Ibid., 206.

7. Ibid., 70.

8. Ibid., 164.

9. Ibid., 113.

10. Ibid., 110.

11. G. L. Newnham Collingwood, ed., *Memoirs of Lord Collingwood: A Selection from the Public and Private Correspondence of Vice-Admiral Lord Collingwood Interspersed with Memoirs of His Life,*

1st American ed. (New York: G. and C. and H. Carvill, 1829), 22.

12. Geoffrey Rawson, ed., *Nelson's Letters from the Leeward Islands and Other Original Documents in the Public Record Office and the British Museum* (London: Golden Cockerel Press, 1953), 23.

13. Ibid., 29.

14. Collingwood, ed., *Memoirs of Lord Collingwood*, 43.

15. Ibid., 130.

Chapter 3. Sea of Contention

1. "Columbus Announces His Discovery," in *Microsoft Encarta Encyclopedia*, CD-ROM, 2.

2. Peter Padfield, *Maritime Supremacy and the Opening of the Western Mind* (New York: Overlook Press, 1999), 276.

3. Nicolas, ed., *Dispatches and Letters of Lord Nelson*, vol. 1, 114.

4. Ibid., 148.

5. Ibid., 11.

6. Ibid., 111.

7. Ibid., 148.

Chapter 4. Local Perspective

1. Nicolas, ed., *Dispatches and Letters of Lord Nelson*, vol. 1, 114.

2. Ibid., 157.

3. Reverend James Stanier Clarke and John M'Arthur, *The Life of Admiral Lord Nelson: From His Lordship's Manuscripts*, vol. 1 (London: T. Cadwell and W. Davis, 1809), 71.

4. Rawson, ed., *Nelson's Letters from the Leeward Islands*, 14.

5. Andrew Jackson O'Shaughnessy, *An Empire Divided* (Philadelphia: University of Pennsylvania Press, 2000), 247.

Chapter 5. Geopolitical Factors

1. Captain A. T. Mahan, *The Influence of Sea Power upon History, 1660–1783* (New York: Dover, 1987), 328.

2. Nicolas, ed., *Dispatches and Letters of Lord Nelson*, vol. 7, 314.

3. Paul M. Kennedy, *The Rise and Fall of British Naval Mastery* (London: Allen Lane/Penguin Books, 1976), 109.

4. "Count-down to the Saints: A Strategy of Detachments and the Quest for Naval Superiority in the West Indies, 1780–2," *The Mariner's Mirror* 87, no. 2 (May 2001): 150.

5. In J. R. Hill, ed., *The Oxford Illustrated History of the Royal Navy* (Oxford: Oxford University Press, 1955), 105.

6. Nicolas, ed., *Dispatches and Letters of Lord Nelson,* vol. 1, 176.

7. Julian S. Corbett, *Some Principles of Maritime Strategy* (Annapolis: Naval Institute Press, 1988), 222.

8. Peter Padfield, *Maritime Supremacy and the Opening of the Western Mind* (New York: Overlook Press, 1999), 273.

9. George P. B. Naish, ed., *Nelson's Letters to His Wife and Other Documents, 1785–1831* (London: Routledge and Kegan Paul, 1958), 10.

10. Nicolas, ed., *Dispatches and Letters of Lord Nelson,* vol. 1, 157.

11. Ibid., vol. 4, 95.

12. Mahan, *Life of Nelson,* vol. 1, v.

Chapter 6. Troubled Waters

1. Nicolas, *Dispatches and Letters of Lord Nelson,* vol. 1, 113.

2. Rawson, ed., *Nelson's Letters from the Leeward Islands,* 27.

3. Ibid., 33.

4. Ibid., 29.

5. Ibid., 34.

6. Ibid., 41.

7. Nicolas, ed., *Dispatches and Letters of Lord Nelson,* vol. 1, 191.

8. Ibid.

9. Ibid., 156.

10. Ibid., 134.

11. Ibid., 178.

12. Ibid., vol. 7, 35.

13. Ibid., vol. 1, 124.

14. W. Clark Russell, *Horatio Nelson and the Naval Supremacy of England* (New York: G. P. Putnam's Sons, 1905), 34.

15. Nicolas, ed., *Dispatches and Letters of Lord Nelson*, vol. 1, 167.

16. Ibid., 115.

CHAPTER 7. LEGAL MORASS

1. Remarks prepared for delivery at the Dallas Trade Mart by President John F. Kennedy, in *The Greenhill Dictionary of Military Quotations* (London: Greenhill Books, 2000), 273.

2. Rawson, ed., *Nelson's Letters from the Leeward Islands,* 28.

3. Naish, ed., *Nelson's Letters to His Wife,* 10.

4. Rawson, ed., *Nelson's Letters from the Leeward Islands,* 29.

5. Nicolas, ed., *Dispatches and Letters of Lord Nelson,* vol. 3, 141.

6. Rawson, ed., *Nelson's Letters from the Leeward Islands,* 29.

7. Nicolas, ed., *Dispatches and Letters of Lord Nelson,* vol. 1, 174.

8. Ibid., 116.

9. Ibid., 135, 159.

10. Ibid., 215.

11. Ibid., 179.

12. Mahan, *Life of Nelson,* vol. 1, 64.

13. Ibid., 65.

CHAPTER 8. THE SCHOMBERG AFFAIR

1. David Walder, *Nelson* (New York: Dial Press/James Wade, 1978), 85.

2. Ibid.

3. Nicolas, ed., *Dispatches and Letters of Lord Nelson,* vol. 1, 209.

4. Ibid., 208.

5. Ibid., 237, 238.

6. Tom Pocock, *Sailor King: The Life of King William IV* (London: Sinclair-Stevenson, 1991), 105.

7. Nicolas, ed., *Dispatches and Letters of Lord Nelson,* vol. 1, 250.

8. From a private collection.

9. This letter is in the Nelson Museum, Monmouth (Ref E540).

CHAPTER 9. FRAUD AND PARDON

1. Mahan, *Life of Nelson,* vol. 1, 79.
2. Nicolas, ed., *Dispatches and Letters of Lord Nelson,* vol. 1, 226–30.
3. Carola Oman, *Nelson* (London: Reprint Society Ltd., 1950), 75.
4. Oliver Warner, *A Portrait of Lord Nelson* (London: Chatto and Windus, 1959), 65.
5. Nicolas, ed., *Dispatches and Letters of Lord Nelson,* vol. 1, 273.
6. Rawson, ed., *Nelson's Letters from the Leeward Islands,* 60.
7. Ibid., 62.
8. Mahan, *Life of Nelson,* vol. 1, 79.
9. Ibid., 81.

CHAPTER 10. THE PREDECESSORS

1. Tom Pocock, *Horatio Nelson* (London: Bodley Head, 1987), xvii.
2. See Tom Pocock, *Nelson's Women* (London: André Deutsch, 1999), for an excellent exposition of the women in Nelson's life.
3. Ibid., 27.
4. Pocock, *Horatio Nelson,* 59.
5. Nicolas, ed., *Dispatches and Letters of Lord Nelson,* vol. 1, 88.
6. Ibid., 92.
7. Geoffrey Rawson, ed., *Letters from Lord Nelson* (London: Staples Press, 1949), 47.
8. Nicolas, ed., *Dispatches and Letters of Lord Nelson,* vol. 1, 119.
9. Ibid., vol. 5, 356.
10. Ibid., 110.
11. Ibid., 124.
12. Ibid., 131.

CHAPTER 11. A YOUNG WIDOW

1. Oman, *Nelson,* 63.

2. For an excellent analysis of the Battle of Santa Cruz, where Nelson's life was saved by his stepson, Josiah Nisbet, see Colin White, *1797: Nelson's Year of Destiny* (Gloucestershire: Sutton Publishing, 1998).

3. E. M. Keate, *Nelson's Wife: The First Biography of Frances Herbert, Viscountess Nelson* (London: Cassell, 1939), 2.

4. Ibid., 18, 19.

5. Nicolas, ed., *Dispatches and Letters of Lord Nelson,* vol. 1, 133.

6. Clarke and M'Arthur, *Life of Admiral Lord Nelson,* vol. 1, 78.

7. Oman, *Nelson,* 65.

8. Naish, ed., *Nelson's Letters to His Wife,* 13.

9. Nicolas, ed., *Dispatches and Letters of Lord Nelson,* vol. 1, 133.

10. Naish, ed., *Nelson's Letters to His Wife,* 13.

CHAPTER 12. COURTSHIP

1. Naish, ed., *Nelson's Letters to His Wife,* 16.

2. Nicolas, ed., *Dispatches and Letters of Lord Nelson,* vol. 1, 144.

3. Ibid., 160.

4. Perhaps the most idealized relationship between a man and woman in literature was that between Adam and Eve created by John Milton in *Paradise Lost,* published in 1667. Given the interest of his father in classical literature, it is quite possible that Nelson had been exposed to that epic poem.

CHAPTER 13. MARRIAGE

1. Naish, ed., *Nelson's Letters to His Wife,* 18.

2. Ibid., 34.

3. Nicolas, ed., *Dispatches and Letters of Lord Nelson,* vol. 1, 203.

4. Naish, ed., *Nelson's Letters to His Wife,* 45.

5. Ibid., 61.

6. Oman, *Nelson,* 351.

7. Nicolas, ed., *Dispatches and Letters of Lord Nelson,* vol. 1, 167.

8. Ibid., 203.

9. Naish, ed., *Nelson's Letters to His Wife,* 352.

10. Ibid., 49.
11. Nicolas, ed., *Dispatches and Letters of Lord Nelson*, vol. 1, 216.
12. Ibid., 219.
13. Clarke and M'Arthur, *Life of Admiral Lord Nelson*, vol. 1, 94.
14. Howarth and Howarth, *Nelson: The Immortal Memory*, 85.
15. Keate, *Nelson's Wife*.

CHAPTER 14. AFTERMATH

1. Nicolas, ed., *Dispatches and Letters of Lord Nelson*, vol. 1, 248.
2. Ibid., 260.
3. Ibid., 259.
4. Clarke and M'Arthur, *Life of Admiral Lord Nelson*, vol. 1, 101.
5. Ibid., 102.
6. Rawson, ed., *Nelson's Letters from the Leeward Islands*, 72.
7. Ibid.
8. Nicolas, ed., *Dispatches and Letters of Lord Nelson*, vol. 1, 248.
9. Ibid., 251.
10. Ibid., 266.
11. Ibid. 11.
12. Howarth and Howarth, *Nelson: The Immortal Memory*, 94.
13. Nicolas, ed., *Dispatches and Letters of Lord Nelson*, vol. 1, 276.
14. Ibid., 281.
15. Ibid., 252.
16. Mahan, *Life of Nelson*, vol. 2, 398.

CONCLUSION

1. Tom Pocock, *Nelson and His World* (London: Book Club Associates, 1974), 126.
2. Nicolas, ed., *Dispatches and Letters of Lord Nelson*, vol. 1, 70.
3. Mahan, *Life of Nelson*, vol. 1, v.

Bibliography

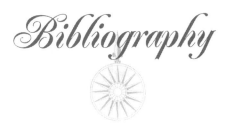

A list by general categories of books about Admiral Lord Nelson follows. It is by no means all inclusive and will, no doubt, become dated as new books about Britain's greatest naval hero continue to emerge during Britain's dedicated Decade of Nelson, which will reach its climax on 21 October 2005. Later editions of some of the best-known biographies are listed. Notable examples include Carola Oman's *Nelson* and Robert Southey's *Life of Nelson*. Works in each category are listed by date of publication, from the most recent to the oldest.

BIOGRAPHIES

The Nelson Touch: The Life and Legend of Horatio Nelson. Terry Coleman. Oxford: Oxford University Press, 2002.

The Life of Nelson. A. T. Mahan. Reprint, Annapolis: Naval Institute Press, 2001. Original edition, Boston: Little, Brown, 1897.

Nelson: A Personal History. Christopher Hibbert. New York: Viking Penguin, 1994.

Nelson, the Immortal Memory. David Howarth and Stephen Howarth. London: J. M. Dent and Sons, 1988.

Horatio Nelson. Tom Pocock. London: Bodley Head, 1987.

A Portrait of Lord Nelson. Oliver Warner. Harmondsworth, Middlesex, England: Penguin, 1987.

Nelson. David Walder. New York: Dial Press/James Wade, 1978.

Nelson, the Essential Hero. Ernle Bradford. New York: Harcourt Brace Jovanovich, 1977.

Nelson the Commander. Geoffrey Bennett. New York: Charles Scribner's Sons, 1972.

Nelson. Carola Oman. London: Hodder and Stoughton, 1947.

The Sailor's Nelson. Admiral Mark Kerr. London: Hurst and Blackett, 1932.

Nelson. Clennell Wilkinson. London: George G. Harrap, 1931.

Lord Nelson, C. S. Forester. Indianapolis: Bobbs-Merrill, 1929.

The Life of Nelson. Geoffrey Callender. London: Longmans, Green, 1912.

Nelson and His Times. Charles Lord Beresford and H. W. Wilson. London: Harmsworth Brothers, 1897–98.

Pictures from the Life of Nelson. W. Clark Russell. New York: Dodd, Mead, 1897.

The Life of Lord Nelson. Robert Southey. 2 vols. London: John Murray, 1813.

The Life of Admiral Lord Nelson. Reverend James Stanier Clarke and John M'Arthur. 2 vols. London: T. Cadwell and W. Davis, 1809.

The Life of Lord Viscount Nelson. T. O. Churchill. London: J. and W. MacGavin, 1808.

BOOKS BASED ON NELSON'S OWN WORDS

Nelson Speaks: Admiral Lord Nelson in His Own Words. Joseph F. Callo. Annapolis: Naval Institute Press, 2001.

The Dispatches and Letters of Admiral Lord Nelson. Edited by Sir Nicholas Harris Nicolas. Reprint, London: Chatham Publishing, 1997. 7 vols. Original edition, London: Henry Colburn, 1844–46.

Nelson's Letters to His Wife and Other Documents. Edited by George P. B. Naish. London: Routledge and Kegan Paul, 1958.

Nelson's Letters from the Leeward Islands and Other Original Documents in the Public Record Office and the British Museum. Edited by Geoffrey Rawson. London: Golden Cockerel Press, 1953.

Letters from Lord Nelson. Compiled by Geoffrey Rawson. New York: Staples Press, 1949.

The Nelson Touch: An Anthology of Lord Nelson's Letters. Compiled by Clemence Dane. London: William Heinemann, 1942.

Memoirs of the Life of Vice-Admiral Lord Viscount Nelson. Thomas Joseph Pettigrew. 2 vols. London: T. and W. Boon, 1849.

Nelson's Era and the Geopolitical Circumstances during His Tour in HMS *Boreas*

The Sea Warriors. Richard Woodman. London: Constable Publishers, 2001.

Maritime Supremacy and the Opening of the Western Mind. Peter Padfield. New York: Overlook Press, 2000.

The Rise and Fall of British Naval Mastery. Paul M. Kennedy. London: Allen Lane/Penguin Books, 1976.

Battles

Nelson and the Nile. Brian Lavery. London: Chatham Publishing, 1998.

The Campaign of Trafalgar, 1803–1805. Edited by Robert Gardiner. London: Chatham Publishing, 1997.

Nelson's Battles: The Art of Victory in the Age of Sail. Nicholas Tracy. London: Chatham Publishing, and Annapolis: Naval Institute Press, 1996.

Sea Battles in Close-up: The Age of Nelson. David Lyon. Annapolis: Naval Institute Press, 1996.

Trafalgar: Countdown to Battle. Alan Schom. London: Michael Joseph, 1990.

Trafalgar and the Spanish Navy. John D. Harbron. London: Conway Maritime Press, 1988.

The Great Gamble: Nelson at Copenhagen. Dudley Pope. New York: Simon and Schuster, 1972.

The Age of Nelson: The Royal Navy in the Age of Its Greatest Power and Glory. G. J. Marcus. New York: Viking Press, 1971.

Trafalgar: The Nelson Touch. David Howarth. New York: Atheneum, 1969.

Nelson's Battles. Oliver Warner. London: B. T. Batsford, 1965.

Trafalgar. Oliver Warner. London: B. T. Batsford, 1961.

The Battle of the Nile. Oliver Warner. London: B. T. Batsford, 1960.

Decision at Trafalgar. Dudley Pope. Philadelphia: J. B. Lippincott, 1960.

The Campaign of Trafalgar. J. S. Corbett. London: Longmans, Green, 1910.

BOOKS ABOUT NELSON AND PARTICULAR SUBJECTS

Legacy of Leadership: Lessons from Admiral Lord Nelson. Joseph F. Callo. Central Point, Ore.: Hellgate Press, 1999.

Nelson's Women. Tom Pocock. London: André Deutsch, 1999.

1797: Nelson's Year of Destiny. Colin White. Gloucestershire, England: Sutton Publishing, in association with the Royal Naval Museum, 1998.

Every Man Will Do His Duty: An Anthology of Firsthand Accounts from the Age of Nelson. Edited by Dean King with John B. Hattendorf. New York: Henry Holt, 1997.

Nelson against Napoleon. Edited by Robert Gardiner. London: Chatham Publishing, and Annapolis: Naval Institute Press, 1997.

Nelson's Mediterranean Command: Concerning Pride, Preferment and Prize Money. Denis A. Orde. Edinburgh: Pentland Press, 1997.

Fleet Battle and Blockade: The French Revolutionary War 1793–1797. Edited by Robert Gardiner. London: Chatham Publishing, 1996.

Nelson: The Life and Letters of a Hero. Roger Morriss. London: Collins and Brown, 1996.

Men-of-War: Life in Nelson's Navy. Patrick O'Brian. New York: W. W. Norton, 1995.

The Nelson Companion. Edited by Colin White. Gloucestershire: Alan Sutton Publishing, and Annapolis: Naval Institute Press, 1995.

Remembering Nelson: A Record of the Lily Lambert McCarthy Collection at the Royal Naval Museum, Portsmouth. As told to Lieutenant Commander John Lea, RN. Published privately in association with the Royal Naval Museum, 1995.

Nelson's Navy. Brian Lavery. London: Conway Maritime Press, and Annapolis: Naval Institute Press, 1989.

The Trafalgar Roll. Robert Holden Mackenzie. Annapolis: Naval Institute Press, 1989.

The 100-Gun Ship Victory. John McKay. London: Conway Maritime Press, 1987.

Sea Life in Nelson's Time. John Masefield. London: Conway Maritime Press, 1984.

Life in Nelson's Navy. Dudley Pope. Annapolis: Naval Institute Press, 1981.

Nelson and the Hamiltons. Jack Russell. New York: Simon and Schuster, 1972.

A Naval History of England. Vol. 2: *The Age of Nelson.* G. J. Marcus. London: George Allen and Unwin, 1971.

Nelson's Last Diary. Introduced by Oliver Warner. Kent, Ohio: Kent State University Press, 1971.

Nelson's Captains. Ludovic Kennedy. New York: W. W. Norton, 1951.

Nelson's Wife: The First Biography of Frances Herbert, Viscountess Nelson. E. M. Keate. London: Cassell, 1939.

The Nelson Collection at Lloyd's. Warren R. Dawson. London: Macmillan, 1932.

Nelson in England: A Domestic Chronicle. E. Hallam Moorhouse. London: Chapman and Hall, 1913.

Nelson and His Captains. W. H. Fitchett. London: Smith, Elder, 1904.

Nelson and His Companions in Arms. J. K. Laughton. London: Longmans, Green, 1896.

Index

Adams, John, 58

Admiralty: on contracting practices in West Indies, 116–17; frigate shortages complaints to, 20; lack of support for geographically-distant captains, 8–9; Moutray–Nelson dispute and, 138; Nelson perception by, 117, 120, 123–24; Nelson's finances and, 184; rates, 22–23; reprimand after Schomberg affair, 112–13; reprimand on Clark's pardon, 122–23; reprimands by, 24–25, 102–3; response to Nelson's Wilkinson and Higgins fraud alert, 119–20; support for Navigation Acts enforcement by, 100

Agamemnon, HMS, 167, 188

Albemarle, HMS, 11, 29, 129, 133; Nelson captures prize ships in command of, 4; prize money opportunities for, 194

American Revolution, British economic growth after, 72–74

Andrews, Elizabeth, 133–35

Antigua, 56–57

Archbald, Sholto, 180

Army-Navy assault at Fort San Juan, Nicaragua, 11

Augusta, Princess of England, 185

authority as second-in-command, 5

Badger, HMS, 11

Band of Brothers, 192

Barfleur, HMS, 29, 109, 132

Boreas, HMS: about, 19–20; delays in paying-off after return to England, 177–78; description of,

Boreas, HMS: (_continued_)
22–24; duel among midshipmen
of, 31; French frigate tour through
West Indies and, 30–31; as frigate,
21; Hurricane Hole and, 27–28; life
aboard, 26; Nelson's peacetime
appointment to, 3, 4–5, 11–12;
Nelson's wedding gift from crew of,
173; performance of, 25; repairs and
maintenance to, 28; runs aground,
6–7; social schedule for captain of,
28–29; voyage to England, 177; West
Indies tour of, 26–27

Byron, John, 39–40

Cape St. Vincent, Battle of (1797), 34, 86

carronades (naval gun), British use
of, 41, 66

Charlestown, Nevis, 57

Charlotte, Queen of England, 185

Chatham, Lord (William Pitt the
Elder), 73, 186

Chesapeake, Battle of, 66–67

Clark, William, 120–22

Clarke, James Stanier, 5, 52–53, 166

Collingwood, Cuthbert: burial of, 35;
Clark court-martial and, 121; the
Moutrays and, 136, 140;
Navigation Acts enforcement and,
33–34; on Nelson, 34; Nelson and,
32–33, 96; on Nelson as Nisbet
suitor, 150; U.S. ship with "emergency" repair need, 79–80

Collingwood, Wilfred, 33, 102; Clark
court-martial and, 121, 123;

colonialism, maritime power and,
38–40

Columbus, Christopher, 37

combat doctrine, Nelson's, 8, 191–92;
resolution in adversity and, 102

Corbett, Julian, 39, 70

Cornwallis, Charles, 66

Cornwallis, William, 5, 185–86

corruption: in Royal Navy, 15; of
West Indies' customs officials,
82–83; Wilkinson and Higgins
allegations of, 115–16

court-martial with death sentence, 5,
120–22; Admiralty's disapproval
of, 122–23

Cromwell, Oliver, 44

customs agents, West Indian, 52; corruption of, 82–83; Nelson and, 85

Davison, Alexander, 131–32

de Grasse, François, 40–41, 66

Denmark, West Indies and, 37

Dutch Indiaman, detention of
Nelson's men by, 7, 8

duty: military definition of, 16–17;
Nelson's definition of, 100; under
pressure, 89–90; to service and country versus marriage and family, 168–71

English Harbour, Antigua, 56, 57

Estaing, Jean-Baptiste-Charles-
Henri-Hector d', 39–40

Fort San Juan, Nicaragua, Army-
Navy assault at, 11

France: Battle of the Saintes and, 40–41; British maritime power versus, 69; national debt of, 41–42; Nelson's animosity toward, 47; West Indies and, 37, 39, 40

frigates, 20–22; "Small Frigates", 22

Gardiner, Alan, 108–9

Gardiner, Robert, 20–22

George III, King of England, 185

gold and precious metals, 37–38

Graves, Thomas, 67

Great Britain: Antigua and Leeward Islands colonies of, 56; Battle of the Saintes and, 40–41; economic growth of, 72–73; France in West Indies and, 43; French maritime power versus, 68–69; geopolitical strategy after Seven Years War, 63–64; global influence of, 65; Industrial Revolution in, 74–75; national debt of, 41–42; naval means of, 65–66; paternalism toward U.S. in, 46; shipbuilding by, 69–71; U.S. in West Indies and, 43–44; West Indies and, 37, 38, 39, 40. *See also* Royal Navy

Grenada, French and British naval fight for (1778), 39–40

Guichen, Admiral, 40

Hamilton, Emma, 51, 131, 187; Jolly court-martial and, 122; Nelson's sense of, 113–14

Hattendorf, John B., 67

Herbert, John, 87–88, 142; first meetings with Nelson, 147; on Nelson–Nisbet marriage, 157–59, 165; Nelson support by, 98

Herbert, Martha, 147

Herbert, Parry, 148–49, 151

heroism, 189–91

Higgins. *See* Wilkinson and Higgins

Hinchinbrooke, HMS, 11

Holloway, Captain, 121

honor, Nelson's, 193–94

Hood, Samuel, 4; appoints Schomberg, 109; Nelson and, 186; on Nelson's censure after Schomberg affair, 112; in New York, 132; responds to Prince William, 110–11; social connections of, 12–13

Howarth, Stephen and David, 17

Howe, Richard, 12, 179

Hughes, Lady Richard, 9–10, 51, 87

Hughes, Richard, 9; love affair of, 155; Moutray command and, 137, 138; Navigation Acts enforcement and, 33–34, 99; Nelson's challenge to, 81–82; as Nelson's military superior, 50–51, 53–54, 100; Ray court-martial and, 121; writings of, 91

Hurricane Hole, St. John, Virgin Islands, 27–28

hurricanes, 56

Îles des Saintes, Battle of, 40–42

Industrial Revolution, 74–75

influence ("interest"), Nelson's, 13–14

Influence of Sea Power upon History 1660–1783, The (Mahan), 63
intelligence, late and inaccurate, 24

Jolly, John, 122

Keate, E. M., 144–45
Keith, Lord (George Keith Elphinstone), 51, 82
Kennedy, John F., 94
Kennedy, Paul, 66–67

leadership: Nelson's, 100–102, 194–96; Nelson's training in, 14, 16, 88–89
Lewis, Michael, 54
Life of Nelson (Mahan), 100
Locker, William, 3
Lowestoffe, HMS, 32
loyalty, Nelson and, 14, 26

Mahan, A. T., 39; on Admiralty's perception of Nelson, 117, 124; on Great Britain's geopolitical situation in 1763, 63; on Nelson's character, 75; on Nelson's duty in Caribbean, 16–17; on Nelson's leadership, 195–96; on Nelson's legal battles over Navigation Acts, 100–102
maritime power, colonialism and, 38–40
M'Arthur, John: on Nelson and Shirley, 52–53; "Sketch of My Life" (Nelson) revision and, 5

Matcham, George, 87
Mediator, HMS, 32, 136
Mermaid-class frigates, 19–20
mission objectives, Royal Navy, 15
Montpelier House, Nevis, 57, 88, 142–43
Moutray, John, 52, 53–54, 56, 135; background of, 136–37; Nelson's dispute with, 137–38
Moutray, Mary, 33, 57, 128, 135–36, 139–41

Naish, G. P. B., 151–52
Napoleon, sea control of West Indies and, 70
naval means: of Great Britain, 15, 65–66; limitations and Navigation Acts enforcement, 58–59; Nelson and, 67, 68; in the United States, 193
Navigation Acts: British maritime power and, 73; Collingwood's enforcement of, 33, 79–80; court challenges to, 92–93; economic problems in enforcement of, 71–72; Hughes's knowledge of, 96; naval means limitations for enforcement of, 58–59; Nelson on enforcement of, 80–81; Nelson's enforcement of, 32, 33, 73–74, 77–78; Nelson's knowledge of, 93–96; terms of, 44–45; U.S. and, 57–58; writ served on Nelson for enforcement of, 183–84

Nelson, Anne, 133

Nelson, Frances Herbert, 57; health of, 181, 182; letters and records about, 174–75; marital unhappiness of, 176–77; on Nelson's duty, 170–71; Nelson's sense of, 113–14; on residing with Nelson's father, 166; voyage to England on *Roehampton*, 177. *See also* Nisbet, Frances "Fanny"

Nelson, Horatio: Admiralty's response to Clark's pardon by, 122–23; Andrews and, 133–35; ascendancy of British naval power and, 42–43; British naval means and, 67, 68; British popular support for, 86; as captain, 24–25; captain's quarters of, 23–24; career influences, 13–16; character of, 113–14; Clark court-martial and, 121–22; coded letters to Fanny, 151–52; Collingwood and, 32–35; Davison and, 131–32; determination of, 98–99; early romances of, 128–29; on half-pay without a ship, 112–13, 186–87; health of, 3, 6, 180–81; heroism of, 189–91; honor of, 193–94; horse bolts with, 10; J. Moutray and, 137–38; J. Nisbet and, 167–68; M. Moutray and, 135–36, 140–41, 151, 156; maritime power for, 75; marriage factors for, 146–47; as monarchist, 45–47, 74, 77, 105–6; on Navigation Acts, 44–45, 46–47; near-resignation of, 178–80; Otway and, 138–39; on potential hostilities with France and U.S., 64–65; previous commands, 11; risk-taking of, 191–93; Simpson and, 129–31; social schedule of, 28–29; U.S. animosity of, 45–46; West Indian colonists and, 49–50; writings of, 17, 90–91

courtship of Fanny: consideration and caring in, 166–67; early letters in, 153–57; financial factors in, 157–59, 165; guileless approach to, 172–73; letters in, 160–62; mail's importance in, 171–72; W. Suckling and, 159–60

duty of: acting first with later approval, 7–8, 24, 31; departure from orders by, 51–52, 72

marriage of, 173–74; children and, 182–83; deterioration of, 187; finances in, 183–84; at Montpelier House, Nevis, 57; Prince William Henry and, 30, 164–65; routine in, 181–82

Schomberg affair: Gardiner detailed to court-martial in, 108–9; Prince William and, 105–6, 113; response to Prince William after, 111; Schomberg's arrest, 107–8

West Indies: Admiralty reprimands after, 102–3; American

Nelson, Horatio: West Indies: (*continued*)

 captains' charges of assault and illegal imprisonment by, 97–98; customs officials and, 85; on customs officials of, 82–83; on general conditions in, 76–77; Hughes's challenge by, 81–82, 94–95; on Hughes's leadership, 84–85; Lady Hughes's support, 87; legal challenges to Navigation Acts, 92–93, 99–100, 151; Navigation Acts enforcement by, 32, 33, 73–74, 77–78; plantation owners and, 85–87; selective vision of, 83–84; Shirley and, 52–53; Shirley's challenge by, 80–81

 Wilkinson and Higgins's allegations, 115–16; action taken on, 119; Admiralty's response to Nelson's actions on, 122–24; letter barrage on, 117–18

Nelson, William, 9, 12, 156

Netherlands, West Indies and, 37, 39

Nevis, 56, 57, 145–46

Newcombe, Captain, 121

Nisbet, Frances "Fanny," 5, 88, 135, 141; description and character of, 144–45; early life, 142; learns of Nelson, 147–48; letters to Nelson by, 171–72; marriage factors for, 145–46; on Nelson's partiality for Josiah, 150. *See also* Nelson, Frances Herbert

Nisbet, Josiah, 132, 143–44, 181; Nelson and, 149–50, 167–68

North, Frederick, 69

Oman, Carola, 143

Otway, Commissioner, 138–39

Padfield, Peter, 41, 70–71

Parker, Hyde, 51–52

Pegasus, HMS: Admiralty on Nelson's orders to, 102; Nelson's orders to Jamaica for court-martial, 108–9; Prince William Henry as captain of, 29. *See also* Schomberg, Isaac

Pitt, William (the Younger), 40, 71

Pocock, Tom, 6, 127, 190

Portugal, West Indies and, 37

Pringle, Thomas, 174

Raisonnable, HMS, 13

Rattler, HMS, 102, 108–9, 120–21

Ray, William, 121

risk-taking, 191–93

Rodney, George, 40, 41, 67–68, 70

Roehampton, 177

Rose, George, 118, 119

Royal Navy: desertion from, 121; Nelson and, 100; peacetime character of, 15; Sandwich's influence on, 69–71. *See also* Admiralty

Saintes, Battle of the (1782), 40–42

St. John's Church, Nevis, 57

St. Lucia and Guadeloupe, 40

St. Vincent, Earl, 132, 188

Sandwich, Fourth Earl of (John Montagu), 69–71

Schomberg, Isaac, 104–5, 106–7

ship shortages, 20. *See also* naval means

Shirley, Thomas: on Collingwood's enforcing Navigation Acts, 79–80; Nelson and, 52–54; Nelson's challenge to, 80–81; writings of, 91

Simpson, Mary, 129–32

"Sketch of My Life" (Nelson), 5, 46, 182

Spain: U.S. changing ship registries in ports of, 83; West Indies and, 37, 39

Suckling, Maurice, 13

Suckling, William, 134, 159–60

sun exposure, deleterious effects of, 31

Syrett, David, 67

Thompson, Horatia Nelson, 183

Trafalgar, Battle of, 65

Turks Island amphibious assault, 132–33

United States: defeat British at Yorktown, 66; naval means of, 193; Nelson's animosity toward, 45–47, 74, 77; Nelson seizes ships of, 97–98; seagoing emergency as cover for West Indies trading by, 78–79; West Indies' customs offi-cials and, 82–83; West Indies trad-ing by, 43–44, 57–58. *See also* American Revolution

Versailles Treaty (1783), 42

Villeneuve, Pierre, 65, 98–99

West Indian colonists: antipathy toward Nelson of, 85–87; on Collingwood's enforcement of Navigation Acts, 80; exemption from Navigation Acts sought by, 96–97; Navigation Acts opposi-tion by, 48–49, 50, 71–72, 78; Nelson's view of, 84

West Indies: Battle of the Saintes, 40–42; civilian and military lead-ership in, 50–52; conflicting authority in, 52–53; early explo-rations and claims to, 37–38; geo-graphical area and conditions of, 54–56; maritime power and colo-nialism in, 38–40; Nelson's tour in, 27; plantation system in, 48; political control during 1784 and 1787 of, 36–37

Whitehall, Miss, 163

Wilkinson and Higgins, 115–16

William Henry, Prince of England, 4; character of, 105, 113; Clark's sen-tencing and, 121; on Nelson and Hood, 109–10; on Nelson and prize money, 194; Nelson as com-mander of, 5; Nelson meets, 132;

William Henry, (*continued*)

the Nelsons' finances and, 185;
Nelson's friendship with, 29–30,
164–65, 169, 173; on Nelson's marriage, 174; Schomberg and, 104–5;
Schomberg's clash with, 106–7;
truce with Hood, 110; on
Wilkinson and Higgins's allegations, 118

Woodman, Richard, 15

Woolward, William, 143

Young, James, 180

About the Author

Joseph F. Callo, whom *Naval History* magazine named author of the year in 1998, has written two previous volumes on Nelson—*Nelson Speaks: Admiral Lord Nelson in His Own Words* and *Legacy of Leadership: Lessons from Admiral Lord Nelson.* His articles on business, travel, and the military regularly appear in leading magazines and newspapers, and his television scripts have earned him creative awards. As a TV producer, Callo helped create award-winning programs for NBC and PBS.

A retired rear admiral in the U.S. Naval Reserve, Callo was commissioned from the Yale University Naval Reserve Officers Training Corps in 1952 and assigned to sea duty with the Atlantic Amphibious Force. Mr. Callo currently resides in New York City with his wife, the former Sally Chin McElwreath, who is a corporate executive and retired U.S. Naval Reserve captain.